HELD IN EVIDENCE

Book One
The Bobby Sherman Miracle

HELD IN EVIDENCE

Book One
The Bobby Sherman Miracle

**Ethel C. Richard
with John Breeding, PhD**

A Well Health Book in Cooperation with John Breeding and
the Coalition for Abolition of Electroshock in Texas.

www.DareToCareToday.com

www.TopShelfPub.com

HELD IN EVIDENCE
Book One
The Bobby Sherman Miracle

The true story behind the US Capitol Historical
Society and NH Historical Society Files

Copyright 2016 Ethel C. Richard
All Rights Reserved.

Published by TopShelf Publishing
an Imprint of: TopShelf Indie Authors & Books, LLC

Although the author and publisher have made every effort to ensure that the information in this book was correct at press time, the author and publisher do not assume and hereby disclaim any liability to any party for any loss, damage, or disruption caused by errors or omissions, whether such errors or omissions result from negligence, accident, or any other cause.

Cover & Book Design
Copyright © 2016 TopShelf Publishing
Book set in 12pt Garamond

Trade Paperback 1st Edition

ISBN: 0-9817619-7-6
ISBN-13: 978-0-9817619-7-8

www.DareToCareToday.com
www.TopShelfPub.com

Additional copies of this book can be ordered from:
Ingram
Baker & Taylor

Acknowledgements

Book One The Bobby Sherman Miracle is named after Bobby because he was there for me and kind to me at a time when I was very young, far from home, in trouble and in serious need of a friend.

Heartfelt thanks to Dr. John Breeding, PhD for permission to reprint previously published material and for his encouragement in this endeavor to educate parents and youngsters about the tragic effects of bullying and gang violence and also about unethical practices in mainstream psychiatry. Special thanks to Richard Young (Founder of Pure Works Foundation) son of Clarence (Tex) and Vera Young (Founders of the famous House of Maranatha, Tucson, Arizona during the late 60's through mid 70's) whose caring mattered at a very critical time and for their cooperation and participation in the presentation of this autobiography, for their written testimony and encouragement and for the use of their photo of House of Maranatha in the logo for this project and for the book. Photo of Bobby Sherman and Wesley Stern during the time of the filming of "Getting Together" and the photo of Cindy

Ethel C. Richard

Williams are reprinted under fair use and are in this book as an aid to tell Ethel's history and her actual associations as well as being cited for educational purposes of children's public education in the fight against youth and gang violence in America. No part of this work may be reproduced without express written consent of the author except to cite within short media clips and in classroom reference. United States Historical Politics, U.S. Presidential Campaigns, Women's Unusual Political Histories and Their Autobiographies U.S.Celebrated Female Public Figures (Public access doctrine and guidelines). Special Acknowledgement and Thanks to NH Senator Lou D'Allesandro (District 20) who saw it fit to recommend my political history to The United States Capitol Historical Society, Washington, D.C. (and) to The New Hampshire Historical Society on May 9, 1996

The Bobby Sherman Miracle

Dedications

Firstly I dedicate this book and this project to The Living God who has always been my close friend and who has preserved me so that my life will be used for good purposes to help others and that this project and this book will be.

This book and the Held In Evidence Series Education Project are dedicated to my mom and dad: Nellie and Andrew Richard, to my brothers: Donald and Edward, to my adult children: Keith-Allen, Jason, Julie-Anne, Catherine, and David, and to my live-in granddaughter, Kathryn, and all my many grandchildren scattered about the country. I'd also like to dedicate this book to Ibrahim, a newborn american boy whose parents are new americans of Pakistani descent, and to all young people around the world, whom I have always wished will grow healthy and with good associations, free of abuse, bullying, and violence within their lives.

Very special thanks to my sons Keith and David who have been of support and assistance in a billion ways throughout this project and to Asad (Ibrahim's dad) who has encouraged this project and supplied important resources to help it become a reality and not just a dream. And a heartfelt thank you to Tom Dae/Frank Draus Jr. (my friend of 48 years who recently passed away without having seen the actual publication of this book and who supported this project whole heartedly).

TABLE OF CONTENTS

Acknowledgements	vi
Dedications	vii
Preface by John Breeding, PhD	11
Introduction	13

PART ONE

Chapter One   19
*Walking Through the Park with Bobby and
The Awakening of a Memory*

Chapter Two   53
The Loneliness of Dark Nights and Cold Rain

Chapter Three   73
Sister St. Phil'eas

Chapter Four   85
*On Moving Too Much, Mr. Petrick and We Clowns
The Neighborhood Referral Office (and)
Eddie Has an Accident*

Chapter Five   97
Family Betrayal, Abandonment and Dr. Koutras

Chapter Six   109
Let's Jump the "S" Monster

Chapter Seven — 113
The Criminality of Professional Mainstream Psychiatry
My views on psychiatry and "mental illness"...

ELECTROSHOCK... — 123
by Dr. John Breeding, PHD

PART TWO

Chapter Eight — 153
Living in a Fear Filled Fog
  Born to be Wild

Chapter Nine — 161
Searching for a Better Life in a Wicked World

Chapter Ten — 177
Bobby Sherman Here I Come...
Ethyle' Gets Together With Bobby Sherman

Chapter Eleven — 201
A Brief Synopsis, Incidents at Denver and Rodney

Evidence — 207

Epilogue — 215

More Evidence — 221

Preface

by John Breeding, PhD

As Ethel points out in the introduction to her book, *"sometimes bad things happens to good people, and we must pick up the pieces as best we can and move on"*. I want to attest here to the fact that Ethel has not only picked up and moved on, but she has lived a wonderful and heroic life. She has been an integral part of her community, raising a passel of children and grandchildren. Ethel was bullied and abused as a young person, experiencing severe trauma at the hands of the people who should have only nurtured and supported her. Then when she was sent to the *"helping professionals"* of our mental health system, that "help" became further abuse in the form of coercive incarceration, poisoning by toxic drugs, and assault by brain-damaging electroshock.

Despite all this abuse, Ethel's natural empathy and compassion was not stilled. Not only did she manage by hard personal work and the healing powers of time to recover enough to take care of herself and her family, but she has also

Ethel C. Richard

never forgotten what she witnessed. That deep and terrible experience has since been strengthened by her research and investigation, so that she now carries a bone deep awareness that psychiatric oppression continues to wreak its damage of the most vulnerable via that trilogy of coercion, drug poisoning and electroshock. The numbers of citizens harmed in the name of psychiatric pseudoscience are astounding. This book is another piece of Ethel's lifework of speaking the truth in service of those she loves, which fortunately includes us all. She is determined to do everything within her powers to help others be the best they can be in relationship, and hopefully avoid some of the treacherous pitfalls posed by the psychiatric system in our world today. I am honored to be included.

The Bobby Sherman Miracle

Introduction

I am much older now and have maturity enough to know that sometimes bad stuff happens to good people and we must pick up the pieces as best we can and move on. Life does not stop and we need to keep up with its challenges. Do I wish that things had gone differently? Everybody has a reason to be here (including me with my hard to deal with history). Hear me clearly. I did not enjoy being attacked and I am totally against violence of all kinds (I even changed my opinion of capital punishment and I am against it now for years). In my circumstances what I feel is right and necessary is that I should try and help others who are possibly facing the same path that my life took when I was young.

My opinion is that I survived and I am living a viable and reasonably happy life and I have an obligation as a decent human being to help others to avoid the horrible trappings of involuntary commitment, forced psychotropic drugs and electroshock. Parents and their kids need to be educated about good communications and affection at home. Kids and

Ethel C. Richard

adolescents need to learn the truth about how to forge and maintain healthful relationships and how to totally avoid unhealthy associations. It seems to me that if I avoid telling the truth about my personal experiences (whether as an electroshock survivor, as a person who was bullied, beaten up and stalked by killers or a kid who had a special past friendship with Bobby Sherman) that some other kid just as frightened, lost, obstinate, desperate and lonesome as I was might fall into similar thinking and circumstances. Receiving electroshock in the hospital for a year was a major factor in the resulting loss of my memory. Maybe another kid is out there and without my story to explain the horrors of electroshock to parents and of life on the road to kids some other kid might put his or her thumb in the air and another nightmare will begin. Only he or she may not be so fortunate that they also survive. If I can help just one kid to stop and face his difficulties and to find a way to get real help to stay safe and to say "no" to the road, I will do it. Sincere thanks for reading my story.

It jumps around a little bit and gets complicated. I've done my best to relate to you folks what happened in precisely the way it really did happen and so I am hoping that the several layers of these events will be easily followed without too much difficulty. Also, some of the perpetrators of the incidents talked about within this report are still alive and at large as well as their family members and I also have family and must take some care to not be too complacent. So, I am avoiding obvious identification of individuals involved in criminal gang activity in Manchester during

1969 through 1971 in the interest of physical safety. In other words I do not cite last names of guilty persons who were gang members whether they've been prosecuted for their crimes or not. A good number of them were minors then and they deserve the right to have made change within their lives and to not be hounded because of past mistakes. The investigation at Denver, Colorado and the events which took place at the St. Andrew's Episcopal Church on Glenarm Place in lower downtown Denver during July of 1971 and which tie into my story are factual and so closely prove injury to myself at that time that I refuse to side track or hide the facts in any kind of so called "political correctness." Law enforcement officials who were directly involved in incidents at Denver and at Tillamook, Oregon as well as Juvenile Officers in my case are correctly named (actual documented proof supplied where possible) and the names of the good people within my life when I was a young person and who are still alive (as well as some who have passed away) and are named within these reports are notified and are aware that they played an integral part in my life and in the truth of my story and they know their names have not been changed and all except Bobby (who was notified in late October of 1994 about this book and who well meaningly suggested that names in my story be changed and who is however clearly referenced in juvenile hospital records and witness statements in my case, which are also backed by other very strong evidence in the case) have agreed (many in writing) to be identified because they know this book is well documented and accurate.

PART ONE

Chapter One

Walking Through the Park with Bobby and
The Awakening of a Memory

Bobby sometimes had been a little stern with me, like when he once told me firmly during lunch, "Forget your cigarette... sit down and eat!"

In the photo he appears wearing a shirt that is similar to the paisley shirt he wore the day we met when we were walking together while talking and sitting together in the park which was on the Screen Gems facility. The shirt I remember was also purple with large white swirls and had a plunging V neck and long sleeves (being thin and silky) and it had a very tight fitting. He also wore a medallion and what looked like a class ring and crisp black pants with black dress boots.

I do not remember what issue the photo was published in but seeing it now it's easy for me to understand why I became so distraught and despondent at our separation when I saw it.

Ethel C. Richard

Laying in my bed at the hospital I thumbed through the pages of a recent issue magazine my parents had brought for me and I remember seeing his photo and reading the words, "Be Good" and that they seemed to jump at me from the page and I got very upset and was inconsolable for weeks... because I could not be with Bobby anymore.

I remember that my parents could not have brought to me magazines while I was still at the State Industrial School (the reform school). They were not allowed to visit me there because I was under observation and my court hearing had not taken place yet. I was in the NH - SIS for only about 10 days.

During the first few days of my stay at the reform school I had gone into some kind of serious seizure and another girl who was helping an aid to restrain me got injured. I woke sometime later to find myself in a locked room. I had no memory of what had happened. After they took me out of lockup I saw the girl wearing a wrist and hand cast and I asked her what had happened to her.

That's when she took me to the aid and together they explained to me that her hand got caught in my mouth when I had the seizure and had been broken.

Because of this the court decided that I would be re admitted to the hospital. (The story of my prior involuntary commitment and fifteen month stay from January 1970 until mid-April of 1971 as an inpatient there is covered in a later chapter). My parents came to visit with me after my transfer to the hospital.

That's when they brought me the latest issues of my favorite magazines. It is absolutely true that when I saw the page with Bobby's photo and his note to "Be good" while lying in my bed in my room at the hospital I cried my heart and my eyes out, touching his photo and missing him and for what seemed like forever and ever.

One thing is certain. I got his message and like always I did my very best to do whatever Bobby told me to do.

It was very difficult being in the hospital where the aids were certain that I was delusional because I was talking sometimes about Bobby and the studios and about how I missed him.

They had not even been told that I had actually been at the studios. They had not been privy to a lot of things about me.

They had not been told that I had been a good student in school and that I'd won the first place in the New Hampshire parochial schools spelling bee competitions at Sacred Heart School a couple of years prior and had been chosen to represent all New Hampshire parochial school fifth graders in the national competitions... or that I had been accepted by the University of Warwick in Coventry, England to participate in the school's theater education program the following year because of my exceptionalism in spelling and my wish to study Shakespeare and theater.

They had not been told that I'd written novels and short

Ethel C. Richard

stories during fourth grade and that I was a well-liked vocalist having been a performer while in school and at local gatherings. They did not know I'd had great grades as a student and was bragged about by my teachers and the dean as an example to other of my classmates. They had no information about my being attacked in Manchester earlier in May of that year or while in Denver, Colorado during the previous July.

Though it appears from the hospital records that they had information that I'd run away from home, they were totally in the dark about me and as to where I'd been and would slight me as if I were imagining things when I spoke of Bobby.

I was being ridiculed and the kids during group counseling sessions were critical of things that I spoke of.

The aids (nurses I'd supposed) had a therapeutic program to bring kids into the norm of what the staff considered acceptable beliefs, ideas and behaviors.

I did not fit in and the staff felt that I was talking nonsense and so I developed a chip on my shoulder.

Nobody in that place believed anything I told them. There was an air of dislike thrown at me by the aids because I could dance and was getting popular for my choreography of dance while hospitalized.

I would get bored at nothing to do while there and so I's stage a show and the other kids loved it and gathered but the adults were critical of modern yoga and jazz movement. They wrote reports that I was behaving in an overly sensuous way. Though I did not remember being attacked in Manchester or at Denver or anything about

The Bobby Sherman Miracle

Sacred Heart School (or anything about my past schooling or my spelling bee champion status or even of my having being accepted into Warwick University Coed Theater Studies Program)... after my return from California and during my second hospitalization, I did still remember having been visiting with Bobby.

I did not remember going to California. I did not remember running away at all. I was in a fog most of the time. I did get fed up with the aids while I was in the hospital and I learned to play a kind of mind game with them.

I got out of that place by pretending to go along. I would lie to the counselors and tell them what they wanted to hear. I started helping out in the kitchen and leading a few sessions with the more popular kids and discussing matters of other kids habits and my own during meetings which was the staff's idea of improvement. They had a point's reward system in place as discipline and so the more you did with chores to help around the place the better.

If you volunteered to work chores you would earn points and could do things like go to the movies outside of the hospital ...and with enough points (which you could also earn by speaking up at staff and patient meetings and being involved to help the other kids) could earn you a discharge from the hospital - and this is what I did to earn release. I guess you could say, I took on the attitude "if you can't beat 'em, join 'em."

When it came to my memory of Bobby I remembered him as very casual and most comfortable, easy going and sweet with a wide smile and big bright blue eyes wrapped up

Ethel C. Richard

in a dark rich tan and with a fresh distinctive scent to his skin that I breathed in every time I brushed his face with my lips.

His hair was full and kissed by the sun and bounced when he walked. His arm stretched out and his hand around my middle felt to me like I was in the most natural, warm and safest place in the world. I'd felt wonderful when I was near Bob and in his attention.

When he occasionally oogled me I would blush and freeze in shyness. Still I was happy and I wanted his touch. No sense in avoiding the fact that I was crazy about him. I could tell when he was in serious thought and distant however I really loved it when he was playful and paying attention to me.

He was very happy and in surprise to see me when I suddenly showed up one early morning in the driveway at the ranch waiting for him. He literally jumped onto his shift and his eyes opened as very wide as he exclaimed questioningly and with a huge and exited smile, "You're back?"

I replied, "You didn't think that I would stay away that long did you Bobby?"

He jumped out of his little yellow pickup truck (I remember seeing the trucks front grill which I believe had a VW though it's been years and my memory of the truck is a little faded) and we had a few photos taken together standing with our arms around each other's middles.

My girlfriend lived just around the corner on West Oak Street very near to the ranch and had brought her camera along for just such an occasion.

She often hung out at the ranch and saw everybody going in and out of the driveway into the studios lots and brought

The Bobby Sherman Miracle

her camera to take pictures there of the stars. She was with me that morning and snapped photos of me and Bobby enjoying the early morning sunshine with a smile, a kiss and a hug. What a sweet memory is within my heart!

So is mine a love story or an illusion of a love that looked real to me between I and Bobby but which I could never requite?

My heart believes love was there though it was far too complicated by the fact that Bob was a celebrity and was also dating others. I had run into another young woman while in Burbank who'd given me a ride to the studios and she had told me unabashedly that she had "balled" Bobby before. (Meaning that they'd had recreational sex). I'd ignored her.

I had not replied to her statement then however I will explain here years later that it had not mattered to me what she'd said because she had no respect (if she had been in a sexual situation with Bobby she was wrong to be so indiscreet about it (if it'd even happened) and because of this I also had no respect for her or her statement. It was my opinion that one ought not to brag about such things as foolhardy uncaring open sex and then expect to be respected.

I and Bobby both had very slim waists (I was 105 pounds, well-built and 5 ft. tall) and he was about 5 ft. and 9 inches tall and so thin that I easily got my hand around his waist). We naturally and easily were matched in personality and in reciprocation. Bobby was in control and I adored him.

The little time we shared together was more than precious to me. The little moments that we shared together seemed magical. I of course because of all these little moments shared

Ethel C. Richard

with Bobby and being an innocent girl at heart I believed that I and Bobby would be involved as more than friends.

I forgive myself for thinking then that we would have under different circumstances eventually gotten married and would still be together today. I was a very young person with a very strong, mature attitude and Bobby seemed to appreciate that.

The young woman (Patti Carnal) whom Bobby did marry was merely a year older than me when he began dating her. Bobby's mom was only 15 years old when she married Bobby's father. So under the circumstances it was not unreasonable for me to believe that I and Bob could have a chance together (especially after we'd already met and he was publicly flirting with me and paying me some obvious attention). A young woman knows when a man is making advances toward her. Bobby liked me. He made it obvious.

However, there was Patti (Bob had kept her a secret) and though not yet married he was I believe wanting to remain faithful to her. My opinion is that Bobby was in a state of "caught in the middle." On the one hand he had pressure of his work and the worry of his career and though I hate to address it here there was an image issue which Bobby was expected to live up to in order to remain popular within the media and with kids as a teen idol. The magazines were overboard with the squeaky clean moral Bobby Sherman image and it did not give to him much room to be himself... a real human being who makes mistakes.

There were concerns over his age (really being a much older man and with a large teeny bopper following) and

The Bobby Sherman Miracle

business demanded every possible dollar which could be eked from Bobby's squeaky clean image. I and Bobby in a very early conversation together actually had a slight tiff because I had realized that he'd been given a character to play in the real world. The fictitious character of 'Bobby Sherman" (presented in teen magazines in order to sell the mags and his recordings to children). I had scolded Bobby for this because I had also bought into the lies about him in the mags and because of those lies I had come to meet him personally at the ranch. (More about this later)

I at first was not at all privy to Bobby's personal life. By that I mean that as far as I can remember, I was not hanging out with him at his home. Bobby had clearly explained to me in private that he could not take me to his home (while we were sitting together talking within the park on studios grounds). He had explained to me that he was staying with a friend and that his house was not yet ready to live in.

Though I remember that I had also been with Bobby off ranch grounds - those memories involved being with him in places such as within a car or while inside his yellow truck. I don't believe I'd met Patti or Bob's mom Juanita. I and Bobby had personal talks and we shared affection together.

I have not said that we shared physical sexual contact.

He bought me lunch, we had a couple little talks about things of life and about sex and he'd sometimes looked at me in odd and sexy ways and other people pointed out to me that Bobby was looking at me when I hadn't noticed. Sometimes he'd be driving and coming around the corner into the driveway of the Screen Gems ranch and I would be street side

Ethel C. Richard

and he would behave in odd ways toward me while he was at the wheel. It was my girlfriend who had tipped me off at first that Bobby had been taking second and third looks at me and had been ogling me from a distance.

You know that song he did called Waiting at the Bus Stop? He did all of that to me. I am the girl of the song. Anyone who begs to differ with me will not make any difference! When I heard the song after my release from the hospital I broke down crying remembering his wave, his wink and his smile in my direction as he drove around the corner near the ranch and the bus stop which is just around the corner on N. Hollywood Way. The entrance into the ranch is on West Oak Street just before it meets N. Hollywood Way. Being young and really loving Bobby very much I took every word and look that I got from him and every bit of affection that he gave to me very seriously. Bobby fell over himself a few times while fumbling when he saw me and I was dressed in hot pants and a little T-top (I was usually barefootin' or in sandals while hanging out at the ranch and Bobby liked it).

From my perspective it looked like things were getting good and it was near impossible for others not to notice that we were shooting looks at each other and that when we were physically standing beside one another Bobby gave off the impression to everyone that we were involved. He teased me publicly. However, it was just not in the cards...and that's why I cried so hard missing him when later in the hospital I saw his photo with the words he'd scribbled. "Be good..." (because I knew). Later, after I was released from the hospital back in Manchester it would prove to be even

The Bobby Sherman Miracle

more unlikely to ever happen that I would see Bobby again. Bobby had sent to me a message through my Los Angeles probation officer (Joan Hancack) to return when I turned eighteen years old. People in Manchester, NH (my home town) would not even allow me to consider returning to California. I was forbidden to return.

My Manchester probation officer (Patricia Blouin) demanded that I get married to Arthur Katsikas immediately when I turned 18 years old. She told me that if I refused I would be placed on adult parole and have an adult criminal record. She told me to forget about Bobby and going back to California.

Like I said, this was totally opposite of the message that I'd gotten from Bobby through Joan Hancack which was, "Go home, be good, get a job, save your money and later when you are eighteen... COME BACK!" (Joan Hancack who had personally spoken with Bobby had put firm stress at the end of Bobby's message in an effort to convey his meaning).

So again I was devastated... being ordered by the probation department of Manchester in my choice of location, my friends and even my mate.

By this time Bobby had married Patty Carnal and I could not remember being in the hospital or my travels across the country. I had problems with my memory and I was not the same girl.

I felt spacey and I was uncaring what my name might be. It seemed like I was just drifting accepting whatever was expected of me.

Ethel C. Richard

The hospital had put me on some very strong drugs and I was basically a zombie when I'd turned eighteen. I was in deep fear and even having hallucinations. I'd been working at the mission house and attending seminary however I could not keep a regular job. Every time I got a job at a factory I was let go within a few days or a couple of weeks because I could not be fast at the work.

Every job was a peace work job and I had dexterity and movement problems and did not see well and simply could not keep up. I worked hard. I showed up on time every day.

I did everything that I was told to do. Still the outcome was the same and I would leave a job crying because I really wanted to keep a job, however the outcome was always the same. A supervisor would take me aside and tell me, "You're not cut out for this job. You are not fast enough and I'm sorry but we have to let you go."

My Manchester, NH probation officer told me that I was being ordered to get married and so I believed that this was the court's order and that I had no choice. I had occasional flickers of memory of being with Bobby but I could not connect them to how I had been with him. I cried fitful tears many times when I did remember Bobby and I wondered how he was and I prayed for him. I was trying to reconcile that I had to get married and be a good wife and a homemaker and I did my damn hardest to be sincere and faithful and plan on a family and family life. I had a lot to learn of being a homemaker so I set my mind to doing just that.

Once in awhile I was lucid enough to have some recall

The Bobby Sherman Miracle

of things that happened between me and Bobby and I called Ward (Bobby's manager) just to say hi and I would ask him how Bobby was and to relay a small message to Bobby for me. Once I had remembered that Bobby had given to me some money and I mailed to Ward for Bobby a small check to pay him back the money he had given to me. These things happened during 1972 and into 1973. My heart was broken over the whole situation but I married Arthur and I had some real nice kids.

The marriage however was doomed from the start. We were just not in any way compatible and I left him during 1980. Our divorce became final in December of 1982.

Note: Throughout my marriage I had no memory of my travels or of the hospital. That's what did not make sense to me. How could it be that I would have memories of Bobby but no memory of how I got to California?

Recently I talked with and asked my ex-husband if he had any clue when he'd met me that I had been in the State hospital or had hitch hiked across the country three times and he explained to me that yes my parents had told him that I'd been hospitalized and had been given electric shock treatments and that afterward I ran away from home and went to California. He had also met with my Manchester probation officer. Though they would all agree that what was done was in my best interests my opinion is very firm. It all smells wrong. It was a dirty, illegal deceptive move.

They should have been honest with me. Unfortunately nobody had told me about my past and I needed to know because I was hurting seemingly for no reason every day. I cried a lot and I could not function well and up until my memory started to come back (12 years after our divorce) and I started to do the research into my past and asking questions,

I would have sworn that he would tell you that he really never knew anything about my past before or even after we'd been married. Outside of a very hushed old rumor that had circulated in the family (told to me by my cousin's son in 2012) that I'd had a breakdown of some sort when I was a kid, my parents were excellent at keeping my past a total secret from me and from extended family members and so no one in our family ever mentioned my past to me and no one except mom and dad (and to some degree Arthur Katsikas) was clear on what exactly had happened.

My memory began surfacing in 1994 and I contacted Bobby hoping he would remember me, however me and Bobby had other difficulties when I returned because he did not understand that I was someone he'd actually known and had spent time with years before and his management had given to him misinformation. The LAPD officers who I'd spoken with in asking to pass a message to him were not exactly enthusiastic about putting me in touch with him and rather gave me the third degree as if the department were doing an interrogation. The attitude of officers there when I spoke with them was hostile. They did not seem to care that I may have a good reason in wanting to speak with him and I was saddened at the way they were so indifferent toward me.

I deal with this subject more in detail within another chapter. Me and Bobby did in fact get to talk on the phone together on Halloween evening 1994 and again a week later on

The Bobby Sherman Miracle

Sunday night and I was waiting after this for another call from Bob the following week when my client passed away and the agency I worked for transferred me to another client's home. I could not get another call from Bob at the prior client's residence and me and Bob had discussed that perhaps we could synchronize on a time to physically meet at a date in the future.

He'd suggested that to me and so I had to make a decision. Things had not gone well on the phone as Bob did not remember me and I had trouble to explain because what I remembered was very fragmented and I felt self conscious talking with him as he was treating me as if talking with a stranger and someone who was just another fan. He sounded more like a salesman than like the Bob I'd remembered. I got through the conversation and resolved to send to him the files and some mail (which he'd agree to receive). Later he was angry because I had sent to him both the files and quite a bit of mail. I admit that I DID SEND TOO MUCH MAIL however it is also true that I was still in recovery from what had happened and that he was given bogus information about me by his management. So we had this tremendously huge misunderstanding and Bobby is not a nice guy when you send long letters after he'd already told you to send only an occasional note and to not "waste" your penmanship.(His words not mine). I am not so harsh in speaking with others as he was to me that day.

To make things worse his management (Ward Sylvester's secretary Christine) had told me in an rude and insulting way during a phone conversation the week prior that I would not be allowed to speak with Bobby unless I paid the office $10,000 (as that is what Bobby gets in an hour for an hour appearance).

Ethel C. Richard

I of course was taken aback and asked her why I would want to pay $10,000 just to talk with someone who had in the past been a friend of mine? She told me if I had anything to send to Bobby that I needed t get an agent. I told her that I am my own "agent" and that I also have been involved in the business as a record company executive/ representative (which I have been) for TDM Music (a record company on the east coast that was founded by my friend Tommy Dae (who used to be a top 40 1960's rock 'n roll artist- Tommy Dae and The High Tensions) and I explained to her that it is not appropriate to treat an fellow production company with such contempt. She got in a worse tiff and she slammed down the phone in my ear. I resolved to find Bobby myself and send him my file. The only reason I'd put agent information into the files that I'd sent to Bobby at his home is because of this statement made to me by Christine that I absolutely was required to have an agent. I took my files to Sherry Robb Literary Agency in Los Angeles (and Sherry who looked at my documents and sat me down. She was firm in her opinion. She told me then..."You cannot write. However, this (what you have put into my hands Ethel)...is a MOVIE!" (More on what happened between me and Bobby during 1994 in my fourth book of the series titled, "The Return."

I worked as a live in personal care attendant looking after elderly hospice patients and quadriplegic patients and I could not just leave when on duty to meet with Bob and so I asked my agency for time off between clients to travel to Los Angeles and visit with Bob for a talk. I was granted permission and so I sent to Bobby a card explaining when I would arrive. I arrived in LA the day before I arrived at his house. I did not have his phone number and so I could not call him to confirm our meeting. I assumed that he'd received my notification and would be expecting me. Later we'll go into the particulars of that day I'd arrived at Bobby's house (by taxi) and what happened there next. Ok now that out of the way, where did I leave off in my story?

Oh yes, during 1995 while staying with my mom I went through my father's old papers while my mom was not home (dad had passed away in September of 1989) and I was dumbfounded to find the old Burbank Juvenile Court Records that my father had stashed neatly away.

Two sets of them that had differing dates and probation officer names and notes.

Reading them hit me like a hammer.

Officer Joan Hancack's name appears in the second document. I remembered her and the message that she said Bobby had told her to give to me the day that I was taken into custody.

Finding the papers was a real breakthrough. I had tangible proof in my hands that I had not been imagining things and that I had been at the ranch with Bobby and what dates I had been taken into custody. Things started to make more sense to me after I found the papers. I told myself that since I had found the Burbank papers that I could possibly find the others that would piece my life together. I began searching to find every person who knew me and making calls to locate old hospital, school records and important documents.

This was so very important to me. I needed to find out who I really was and what had happened in my life that I could not remember and for some reason nobody wanted to tell me about. My memories had started to resurface during 1994 and they were scrambled and terrifying at first and over time since then I have regained a lot of my childhood memories. I sometimes wish that others would for a moment try to put themselves in my place.

Life is very difficult when you do not even understand your own medical history.

When I was married I had a horrible time living with a man who couldn't even begin to understand me. I hated drugs and partying. He on the other hand lived to party. I did not like his friends or his attitude and he kept getting into trouble. How could I be stuck in such a mess?

Did I make a decision to marry that man? I had not. The probation department had decided for me. Why would they rather ruin my life with a not so great choice for marriage instead of allow me my liberty to choose for myself? What had happened to make me so much different from other persons? There are huge disadvantages to being forced into marriage. People have it rough enough in marriage even when they want to marry one another and feel real love and loyalties. Forced marriage is a horrible fate.

You feel locked into an inescapable loneliness when you are incompatible and when morality and ethics are not the same between two persons how can there be unity? You're instead guaranteed a very painful tour into an existence that is most miserable. The following is an example from my own personal experience.

One morning while I was at home watching after our first

child Keith (who was only a year old) an officer came to our door and showed me 13 bench warrants for MY arrest.

Arthur was not home at the time and I was very upset because my husband had registered the family vehicle into my name (I did not drive a car. I did not even know how to drive and I had no driver's license) and then he'd driven the vehicle around committing all sorts of mostly petty and a couple of major violations and offenses (like breaking and entering and theft).

I was fortunate the officer realized that I was not the culprit who did those things and he asked me to show up at court the next morning for a hearing. The judge was none too pleased with Arthur's behavior and he told me in the courtroom that he wanted Arthur in front of him and that he would "do some time." The entire incident somehow got swept under a rug by Arthur's attorneys. It hurt a lot to live under those kinds of circumstances.

Things escalated and Arthur (who had a serious multi drug abuse problem) became very unstable and more abusive. He became physically abusive to me and was peddling hard core drugs within our neighborhood (to kids) for which I hated him.

Cocaine and LSD are hard core drugs and I could not stand pot and abuse of alcohol either and so it was extremely tough for me to live with Arthur and to watch all of that crap that he was doing. It was even worse than this when it came to our neighbors and I had to thwart anonymous lit quarter sticks thrown into my windows (firecracker explosives which terrified my family- thrown into the house at my babies and

Ethel C. Richard

our tires slashed) and my small children's eyes were being hit with sand by other kids while out to play (my kids were from one to six years old) which things were thrown on purpose by neighbors who hated my husband because he'd sold drugs to their kids (12 year olds). I could not blame my neighbors for being angry however they were monsters to take it out on my babies. They'd argued with me that what Arthur did was also my fault because I was his wife and I was protecting him from them. So I suppose I should have let them pelt him into the ground when 30 or so neighbors piled on him Easter Sunday 1982 (instead of getting involved to stop them) because they would afterward take it out on my small children, slash our tires, break into our home, destroy our belongings and ejaculate (sorry but there's no other words I can use that are not just as offensive that depict the truth) on all of our walls... all because they hated Arthur for what he had done and me as well because I had called the police to protect him from being killed by a mob of crazed angry neighbors in front of his own kids on Easter Sunday.

Who called the police? I did when I realized that those people would kill him. There was no possibility of any type of so called fair exchange. Thirty people on one can do a lot of damage. Was the angry mob that literally grabbed and dragged Arthur out into the parking lot behind the house directly in front of our babies (who were hysterical with crying at seeing their father being punched and dragged across the pavement) thinking about justice or about our kids when they ripped Arthur from our back door to pile onto him with punches?

The Bobby Sherman Miracle

I hated Arthur too... however I was not about wanting to see him get ripped apart by neighbors in front of our kids. I really loved my kids and I tried to help him straighten out for them but eventually I couldn't take it anymore and after the birth of my last child (each of my five children were born by cesarean section) and myself suffering from a serious relapse after having nearly died from a ruptured uterus, upon my doctor's advice (he told me that I would die if I stayed in that extremely stressful relationship) I allowed the doctor to set me up with an appointment for some counseling and support help to actually leave Arthur. It was really tough because I have old fashioned values and believe it's important to stay married and keep the family together through problems and not to bail out.

I was 23 three years old and had already had five children by C-section, had been hospitalized in invalid status and two of our children were severely multiply handicapped.

I was looking after my children by myself as Arthur was gone much of the time. My obstetrician had pleaded with him that I needed to stay in the hospital for about three months to get blood transfusions and gain my strength. The law in N.H. then required a husband's guarantee of payment whether with insurance or by some other method and also his permission for his wife to remain hospitalized for an extended period of time after a birth. Arthur refused for my hospitalization to continue and told the doctors that my mother would watch over the children and take care of our home while I would stay in bed. My doctor arranged for blood transfusions during my last couple of days in the

Ethel C. Richard

hospital and he made it clear before my discharge he did not want me to even pick up my newborn David as he was concerned about the state of my uterus.

After about seven months at home resting I thought I might be well enough to take a small trip 18 miles away to visit with some musician friends of mine who were playing a gig one Saturday night at a hotel in Nashua. I left the kids with my husband and took a taxi to the hotel. There was a huge blizzard that night and when I called a local Nashua Taxi for a ride the cab driver would not take a personal check.

My friends had already left and so being about Two AM I called my husband and told him that I was stuck at the hotel without a ride.

He told me to get a hotel room and I tried to do that however the hotel desk clerk refused my check (he wanted a credit card) and so I called my husband again and he told me that he could not help me. When I got off the phone the hotel clerk asked me to leave and so I left the hotel and I was worried wondering how I would get back home. I ended up walking the eighteen miles home from the hotel using the breakdown lane of the highway. I was totally exhausted when I arrived home sometime during the afternoon the following day. I got into my door and collapsed onto the sofa and immediately my husband was furious. He yelled at me saying something that I don't remember except for some four letter words. He stormed out of the house leaving me alone with the kids. My mom was not there and the kids were hungry and the dishes piled up and the baby needed changing and a feeding. You get the picture?

The Bobby Sherman Miracle

After a couple of hours I collapsed from a huge stabbing lower abdominal pain while holding my tiny David. I managed to hang onto him as tightly as I could to protect him from my fall and I set him down gently onto the floor and crawled to the wall at the opposite side of the room struggling to reach the phone which was up on the wall and I managed to grab it and call my cousin who got my dad to come and bring me to the emergency room.

This all happened over Valentine's Day 1980. My David was then seven months old. Mom took the kids home with her because I was back inside the hospital. I was in the hospital for a few days when three doctors came into my room and explained to me about my illness and that I had to leave whatever was causing my stress at home or I would die.

They did not tell me that I would get sicker. They made themselves very clear. They used the word DIE. My doctor then informed me that he was making an appointment for me for counseling and help to leave my husband before things got worse. During my hospitalization my mom watched the children. My husband who was not around much didn't care to hear what had really happened and did not care that I was in the hospital. He did come back to the house however while I was in the hospital and when I went back he was there.

Arthur found out that I was seeing a counselor and he went to our church and told the clergy a lie that I had cheated on him with another man because I had listened to my doctor and had found a couple of good friends to spend time with who were not involved with drugs and violence (my musician friends one who was a man I trusted that I'd met years before

Ethel C. Richard

when I was 12 years old and who had owned a teenage nightclub in the area, and the other was the female vocalist that he worked with).

I and Arthur had gone out one night to listen to a band at a fancy convention center at the local Sheraton while I was about 8 months pregnant for David and his was the band that was working there that night. He recognized me from years before and came to our table and struck up a conversation with us. We later connected and I and he became good friends and remained close friends for many years until his death February 6, 2015 at 72 years old. He was Tom Dae (also known as Frank Draus Jr.) He was great for moral support and had some good practical advice as well. It was he who taught me to pull myself up and out of the mud and take care of my personal business in an effective way. I love him like a brother and we have spent many hours in conversations over the years. I worked with him later after my divorce for a couple of years when he owned and operated a popular nightclub in northern Maine on the Canadian border. I shared with him what was happening to me when my memory started coming back and I spoke with him from Los Angeles after Bobby and I had the misunderstanding in December of 1994.

Arthur has always been very negative toward my friendship with Tom and Karen and he made a huge stink about it (even getting me excommunicated from our church in 1980 when he found out that I was leaving him and that my friends were providing me moral support to feel better about myself and my decision). It never went beyond friendship but you could not convince my husband.

Let's go back to my explanation of my mental state back then as regarding what had happened to me while on the road and as a result of many factors including my then severely repressed memory of places I'd been and persons I 'd known including those of of Burbank, California and of Bobby.

While I was in my marriage I would sometimes be watching after my kids and in secret remembering Bobby and wondering how he was. It all felt strange to me that I could be married with kids and in a bad marriage and thinking about times I had with someone else from my past that I simply could not connect to in the sense of remembering how we'd met.

I would go to sleep back then and have dreams about being with him. In my dreams there was a recurring theme that I know where he was but that there was an impenetrable unnatural separation between us which should not exist. I had dreams about his house and a red truck and high bushes.

I also had nightmares about being attacked by strangers and people with guns and long tunnels which ran under buildings, hallways and big locked steel doors. I realize now that the dreams were my memories of several events which were trying to push through and as it turns out the tunnels actually exist. They are the tunnels which run under the NH State Hospital Buildings. There are many hallways and big doors that were kept locked when the hospital was in operation. I had in fact while on the road been attacked by strangers and harassed by people who used guns just as I had also really been in Bobby

Ethel C. Richard

Sherman's company those many years ago.

So the issues coming out in my evening dreams had a basis in reality but I could not connect the dots. I had shared some wonderful moments with Bobby and we had been separated (at least from my point of view) under unnatural and heart wrenching circumstances which were interwoven within my memory alongside other very frightening events. The years have passed and now walls of a different nature need to come down. Forty four years is a very long time and people live through a lot as time passes.

My friend Tom back when he looked over my documents (just before I drove the documents to Donald Kennon at Washington, D. C. in May of 1996 and from there continued out to Denver to file lawsuits against the City of Denver and the Colorado Episcopalian Diocese (story in a later chapter) had advised me to be very careful with the information because as he said to me, "You could be opening a terribly fierce can of worms." He knew me very well and he knew that the documents and information in my files as well as my story and the witness statements within it are real.

I want to sturdy my focus here to tell the story of what happened to me when I was a girl and the reasons why it is so important for persons to learn the lessons of my story and to help those of us who are working to abolish the evils of mainstream psychiatry and to find ways to supervise those who are in charge within our juvenile system.

Forcing a young person into an unwanted marriage is an evil practice that leads most often to disaster. I wish people could learn from my experience and avoid some serious

The Bobby Sherman Miracle

heartache in life. This country's people must because of mainstream psychiatry's agenda and its continuing existence police those who hold the keys of authority over our youth and also those who hold control over psychiatry and the psychiatric drug industries. Until they no longer exist as an influential entity they will always be a serious detriment to the health of persons placed under their control. Psychiatry is a pseudo-science and not a medically proven science. It is based on opinion and conjecture and oppresses persons for profit.

We need to institute by way of legislation adequate controls over the deceitful, destructive and illegal activities of the pharmaceutical and electroconvulsive shock machine industries which seek to empty people's pockets while indiscriminately poisoning our communities, our elders and our children with unnecessary and harmful drugs and frying person's brains, creating brain damage and serious neurological impairment in persons and then all in the name of benevolent medicine.

Mainstream Psychiatry, psychotropic medications and ECT are the biggest scam of the 20th century which is currently still perpetrated upon our citizens. Much investigation has been done into the roots of mainstream psychiatry and its founders. Physical lobotomy still exists with changed methods and is now called psycho surgery.

During the mid to late 1950's pharmaceutical companies began developing various psychotropic medications which could supplement or replace prefrontal lobotomy within the institutions with the new chemical replacement for lobotomy having been touted as it's (then) latest cure for mental illness.

Ethel C. Richard

Electric shock (ECT) and the use of such drugs as Thorazine are in its effects as those of prefrontal lobotomy and yet electric shock has continued in use. Use of Thorazine creates a chemically induced lobotomy and other neurological impairment such as tardive dyskinesia and these need to be avoided like the bubonic plague. Those who are familiar with the effects of electroshock understand that without anesthesia the convulsions created are enough to break bones.

Psychiatry has found a way to make persons more receptive to the idea of electro shock as being safe by applying anesthesia at the same time as administration of the shock (which subdues the reactive bodily convulsion) but the shock itself applied to the brain creates a serious closed head injury (though it's not one as outwardly apparent as broken bones) which in repeated administration is cumulative and which even in single administration has the same effect... (Brain damage) and brain damage is not a cure for any ill.

Its use in any creature in nature to control behavior and especially in human beings is a complete abuse and a shameful misuse of electrical power. It is legal systematic designed destruction of a human being and it is known fact and proven that ECT is purposely used by psychiatrists to disconnect an individual's memory function and his personhood in order to ease his "symptoms" of emotional distress and (by whoever dictates) unwanted behaviors... and yet this practice is sanctioned and supported by our tax dollars which we pay into such programs as Medicaid.

Dr. John Breeding, PHD Psychologist has retagged a phrase: that (ECT) is "electroconvulsive terror". For those

The Bobby Sherman Miracle

who don't know…electric shock machines were used by Hitler's Germany when all Germany's psychiatrists by commissioned order of the furor and some rogue American psychiatrists took part in creating electric shock machines as torture devices for use against enemies of Nazi Germany and later those who performed its administration were prosecuted by offended nations for atrocities against humanity.

Dr. John Breeding explains, "Electric shock is large numbers of milliampere, large numbers of voltage of electricity sent directly into the brain crashing through the blood brain barrier, sending toxic into the brain creating cell death by that, creating cell death by the mechanical and heat damage of large voltages of electricity in the brain, creating excito toxicity of adrenal corticoids and other substances in the brain that happen during convulsions that create cell death. We have an estimated 100,000 people each year in this country that are being administered electric shock.

A large percentage of those people end up on permanent disability unable to work at the jobs and professions that they had before. To call electro shock benevolent medicine is basically a complete perversion and twisting of the words benevolent medicine. It's really very appropriately called psychiatric assault. It always causes brain damage. Anybody who tells you differently is either severely misinformed, overtly lying or both. That's the bottom line on electroshock.

And that's called therapy?

Electro convulsions create cell death; sometimes create a temporary euphoria, create the effects of a closed head injury. It disables the brain and central nervous system in a way in

Ethel C. Richard

that it is considered to be therapeutic when somebody is more subdued and disabled and therefore less aware of their problems or temporarily jolted out of them.

That's electro shock. There's nothing pretty about it.

It's a crime against humanity, an assault upon the brain, it always causes brain damage and it's the brain disabling principal of psychiatry that you disable the brain and that is, the "therapeutic effect." (Quote used with permission of Dr. John Breeding PHD psychologist).

The blame for the neurological damage and long term memory loss of which I am a survivor I believe rests solely on the shoulders of the deadly and irresponsible mainstream psychiatry which was practiced by my so called private psychiatrist who saw me for 10 minutes when I was 14 years old and then committed me to NH Hospital - who was also as it turned out to be the superintendent of N.H. Hospital (Christos Koutras). He was angry because I had mouthed off at him and I told him that he was stupid and that I did not want to take the pills he'd prescribed for me (which I did not need).

At fourteen I never smoked a joint or took illegal pills. I had taken a half beer once or twice. I took an aspirin occasionally. I knew that he was not interested in anything I had to say to him and so I did not want anything to do with him or his pills. I did not need his pills (it was not like I had a physical illness and needed a drug like penicillin). I was simply reacting to a bad situation at home and an evil minded bunch of kids who kept bullying me and telling me things about themselves that I simply had no choice but to make a complaint /report to the police (I think that a boy talking with me about having murdered some poor kid qualifies for me to have a talk with the detectives) and that the police would not investigate my complaint and that I got angry because no adults would listen or investigate my complaint did not mean that I should be told that I was ill and then be forced to take drugs…and what of the boy who'd told me of what he and his "friend" had done? He was killed and other boys put into a hospital in critical condition and kept in traction for months.

All of this very sick and true outcome for those boys would perhaps never have happened if the police officers I'd originally contacted in making my complaints back then would have taken my complaint seriously.

I believe that when a medication is unnecessary or makes a person feel ill that it must not be forced upon him. I had not belonged in the State Hospital and yet I'd been committed by a psychiatrist and I'd spent nearly a combined two years there as an adolescent inpatient while being abused by staff and poisoned with the psychotropic so called "medications" of the day and admitted into the hospital's "therapeutic program" which included electroshock.

Because I did not want to take the pills he gave to me Koutras had involuntarily committed me to N.H. Psychiatric Hospital and over the course of a year and three months, the hospital staff pumped me full of Mellaril and Thorazine and they regularly attached me to an electric shock machine. I had to survive the experiences of the mental hospital and then after release I had to survive the crazy people in my

Ethel C. Richard

neighborhood who were running around and killing people, setting others on fire, beating people up, crashing cars, raping girls, intimidating the neighborhood cops and robbing elderly folks. I am so happy that it really is over and that now I live in a reasonably peaceful environment.

I cannot blame myself for what happened to me because when I was a kid I was only trying to survive and looking for some good people to share life with to build a good life and real happiness. At the time I was visiting with Bobby in Burbank he and Patti were not yet married and Bobby had not let on to me that he was involved in a relationship with someone else… and so my visits with Bobby in my opinion were relatively innocent as no sexual/physical relationship that I can remember materialized between us other than small caresses and kisses or a hug here or there and some private talks while sitting and some walks together which I treasured.

As a young and impressionable person then who actually had been visiting and talking with Bobby on a personal level it makes sense that I was not crazy to pursue what looked to me back then as a real chance for love with a man who I believed from my experience with him had good moral character, who had many similar interests and hobbies to mine and was easygoing and fun to be with.

Like I've already said I had not know of Patricia then if I had known of her I would not have pursued his friendship or had those personal talks with him in that way. It was because I believed that Bobby was sincerely interested in me then that I had returned to visit with him the times after our first meeting and so that's how I'd chosen to remember Bobby—

The Bobby Sherman Miracle

as he was when he was happy to see me and to be with me and he was being good to me and was affectionate with me.

I told myself way back then when I was still in the hospital the second time as a girl after having spent time with him over that previous summer that one day should I ever see Bobby again I would explain those things I hadn't when we'd been visiting together. I would tell him I love him.

He can tell you, for right or for wrong doesn't matter because that's just what I did. Whether he understood my meaning (or didn't), I simply had to verbalize what I could never forget (and which he'd started years before in first giving to me a kiss) whether he could or he could not remember doing it. He'd first asked me for a kiss and then he'd kissed me. Bobby was always lovin' on me when I was with him and being young I believed in it and especially when I never saw him greet another girl in the same way he greeted me. So, I fell for him. I was hooked.

Chapter Two

The Loneliness of Dark Nights and Cold Rain

"God, where am I…? Is it 2 AM? …The sky has opened on my head with buckets of cold pouring rain and I want to get warm. I am frozen cold and I am so scared. Is there any place I can stop and rest and forget this day? I have been up and traveling for a long time today and I do not know where I am. Please God protect me. I hate this life and I wish I had a home and a bed with a pillow and a blanket to keep me warm and a hair brush. But I guess that's ok. Just keep me alive and keep me safe. Please be with me because I really need you and I really love you. You're all I have God. You're all I have."

God was my constant companion while I was on the road. I had no jacket and only one set of clothes (a pair of jeans, a thin shirt and a pair of sneakers). No socks. My clothing was very basic with no planning for weather. I had

Ethel C. Richard

my bible (to me it was essential to carry a King James Version of The Holy Bible) which I loved dearly. I carried a dime in my pocket in case I wanted to make a phone call, cigarettes and a highway map of the United States. Looking back at myself then, I realize how my thought process was totally illogical. I had no money... just a very strong belief that I had to turn my back on Manchester and the people there and restart my life far away from trouble and hurts of my past.

Jack had given to me the map on which he'd routed for me the highways to follow to get to Tucson, Arizona. We'd been talking for several weeks about the House of Maranatha and that the people there were nice and caring and would give me a place to stay with them for a while. Bible Studies and prayer meetings... I'd attended many of them. I knew the Bible inside and out. Jack had been converted to Christianity through a fellow named Paul Carter after his service in Nam. Jack had problems dealing with his Vietnam experience. His stories of the nightmare of the war and of his platoon being killed and his sad tales of having to shoot kids who carried live grenades on the orders of their mothers to kill American soldiers was really tough on him.

Jack had turned to drugs in his pain and then later got off the drugs when he became a Christian. Carter had spent time at the House of Maranatha and soon Jack followed. For a time while we were friends then Jack stayed in the basement under my room on Fourth Street (which house was directly across the street from Sweeney Park where the street gangs congregated on a daily and nightly basis).

Jack got access to the basement because I had snuck

him in when he was homeless and he'd been my friend. Jack was able to hear everything being said and going on inside our family's' apartment and so he heard the arguments and he saw how the gangs were always hanging around in front of our building. Jack routed my map because he believed that I would be better off in Tucson, Arizona with Tex and Vera than to be at Manchester bullied by the gangs and with my parents.

The day before I'd left Manchester I was beaten unconscious by gang members and left lying on the pavement in the park. The gang was angry because I told them I was leaving Manchester and that I did not want to deal with all this gang crap or the others in the neighborhood who were too dumb to know to stop the garbage and to make Manchester a good place to live. I told them that I did not feel at home with them or my parents and that I could not be persuaded under any circumstances to stay.

I had already found out about one of the girls who'd been set on fire with lighter fluid by her boyfriend. I had been treated very badly by the gang members myself. Though at that time I did not remember about Charlie and of the secret he'd told me before his death or my having been in the hospital for a year and three months and of recently having been released, I still had plenty to be afraid of in Manchester. (We'll tell about Charlie in a later chapter).

In May of 1971 The female gang leader (April) who pretended to be my girlfriend, was a heavy set girl with muscle who my uncle Ray (who had tried to take me to bed) had told me was hanging with (having an affair with) my dad

Ethel C. Richard

and "doing it" with him, (and so Ray asked me, what was wrong with he himself taking up with me and he giving to me money... seeing that dad was messing with my girlfriends)? My mom had already told me to watch out for Raymond and I became very angry with my uncle, threatening to tell his wife what he was doing and ordering him to leave me alone. I did not believe what he'd said about my father and from that point on I remembered what mom had told me about Raymond and so I told myself I would turn him into my dad who would decide what to do about his own brother.However things did not work out the way I'd planned. April later had hit into me (with her fist) ordering me to stay at home because she didn't want me to "upset my dad" (after I'd told her I was leaving Manchester because I could not stand living there with all the garbage and trouble going on with the gangs). She was my age and I totally detested her and after what Ray had told me about her and my father I paid closer attention to find out if there had been or was contact between April and my dad. I opened my eyes to what she and my dad were doing.. (I hadn't believed my uncle until after I'd tried to tell dad what his brother had done to me and what he'd said to me. The shit hit the fan because I saw my dad walking with April and they talking together from a distance and I began to wonder what my father was talking about with her.

Then the hurt really came down on my head when I confronted dad in front of mom and dad refused for me to even speak of his brother to him in the way I was speaking and in telling him the truth of having been approached for

The Bobby Sherman Miracle

sex by his brother and the things his brother had told me about him (dad) and my girlfriends. The day I got attacked again (before I ran) the entire gang both male and female had gathered on the park pavement in a circle around me closing off the area. I got pinned down and I took a lot of punches but it was the last time that I had to deal with them.

I was beaten into the pavement but I was not even caring about it or thinking about it when I took to the highway the following afternoon.

I called it my independence day. I noted the day right down to the exact time so that I would never forget the date. It was Friday May 14, 1971 at precisely 4 pm.

I used the dime in my pocket to call my mother from Connecticut hours after I'd left Manchester but the dime was not enough and I had to make the call collect. Mom begged me to come home. I told her that I simply could not come back, (I hadn't told her what Raymond had done) that it was time for me to go and that this was how I chose to live my life and that I was old enough to be on my own. I told her that she could not understand but that it was very important that I leave. My mother told me that she was sorry but she could not afford the collect phone call I'd made to her and that she had to hang up. I told her not to worry.... I asked for my brother Eddie and when he came on the phone I told him that he could have all of my LP'S and my electric guitar and amplifier which had been my second most loved possessions (as it was his 13th birthday in just a few days) and so I wished him a happy birthday. My father kept yelling at Mom to get off the phone because he could not afford the phone bill and

Ethel C. Richard

so I said goodbye. The people I had hitched a ride with were bringing me through to Providence, Rhode Island and had made an overnight stop in Connecticut. We arrived in Providence the following day.

I got to go to the Providence Mall and I thoroughly enjoyed seeing the architecture of the building.I stayed with an Italian family in of course the Italian side of town. Nice folks. I moved on the following day. Some folks I met were extremely nice and told me how much the admired my gut to live the way that they wished they had when they were young. Lots of nice people who fed me and some gave to me money to help me survive.

There were those who were not so caring though and even dangerous and I spent my time being as careful as I knew how in order to avoid trouble. I got cornered a few times but was able with God on my side and my wits to get away and I did not have much memory to speak of while traveling.

I lived one moment at a time. I had some things that I wanted to do. I wanted to make it safely to Tucson and I also had in the back burner an idea that I would like to meet and get to know Bobby Sherman. I liked the things I had read about him. He seemed to have lots of the same interests as me. He was interested in psychology and I loved studying psychology and psychiatry. He liked photography and I was also very interested in photography.

He was into music and I was into music. He is a singer and I was a singer too. I'd studied voice and I was very good at it. I was known for my vocals when really young at Christmas events and at school. I was learning guitar and

The Bobby Sherman Miracle

wanted to learn drums. I worked hard in grade school and I got excellent grades. I wrote screenplays, skits, short stories, lyrics and poetry.

In fifth grade I was a spelling bee champ. I had it in my head that I was a really good person and that Bobby looked to be a really good person too. I was sick of all the creep guys in Manchester and Bobby seemed so gentle and nice from the articles I'd read about him. Bobby also seemed to me to have excellent moral character and it all round looked to me like he would be the most compatible with someone like me and me with him. I wasn't really thinking about his career or his particular look. That stuff did not matter to me.

I cared about that maybe we could really hit it off together and that if I did not go for it that we would never possibly meet.

The magazines all told a story that he was single and not involved with anyone in particular. He was different from all the other people I knew in that he seemed like a serious and good hearted man. It felt like it was the absolute right and good thing to do to try and meet him and see where it would go. I had to go to LA. I told myself and I told God in my prayers that with his help I was going to meet Bobby Sherman. My dad when I told him that I liked Bobby yelled at me and told me to stop chasing a married man. I told my dad that all of the magazines say that Bobby was not married but dad was angry anyway.

Truth is at that time Bobby was perhaps in a relationship but was not yet married. His and Patties marriage certificate is dated September 28, 1971. I had met Bobby in June.

Ethel C. Richard

Bobby was not married at the time I was visiting with him. I knew this already in my heart. I was very upset and would not listen when my dad yelled at me about Bobby. Moving ahead in my story briefly let me make it clear that nearly a month later after already having met with and spent time with Bobby and after being flown back to New Hampshire the first time by the Los Angeles Juvenile Court I was allowed to return home with my parents and in the car and on the way to my parents home I tried to talk with my dad about Bobby and the studios and dad totally blew up at me in anger and told me to "shut up" and started a huge argument with my mom. I firmly decided right then and there that I was in a horrible and uncaring place. I never said another word but plotted to be back in Burbank at Bobby's side within the week.

I left again the very same night after having been caught the first time that same afternoon trying to hitch a ride out of town. I was absolutely determined to get back to Bobby at the studios. At that point I had decided that Manchester and my father's home was in no way whatsoever my home.

I got out of there so fast you could probably see me run with flames on my heels. I had not realized however that I had a court date coming in Manchester and that I was still on probation with the courts. It just had not occurred to me. It would not have made a difference anyway. The only thing that mattered to me was to be with Bobby where I felt at home and happy and secure when he put his arm around me and when he asked me for a kiss. I lived for that smile and his quiet nature. Everything just felt so good and so natural and right. He goofed off a little and was fun. I just totally adored him. We were not doing anything wrong at all. I just felt as though I had found myself and I had just the most wonderful times when I was sitting near him or even just when we were walking and talking together.

I was kind of shy and I could not see very well having a blind right eye and poor sight in my left. I have a lazy eye within a locked muscle so it is not noticeable unless you know what to look for. I would never wear glasses because I did not want to appear strange. No contacts either. So not being able to see Bobby very well and not wanting to let on that I was blinder than sighted I took every opportunity to use my other senses when I was near him. When Bobby would ask me to kiss his face I would brush my lips across his cheek in such a slow gentle caress that I would purposely breathe and drink in the scent of his skin deep into my memory. To this day I remember the feel and scent of his face under my lips and nostrils as I kissed him. I breathed in his breath. I would have jumped inside of him if I could have. I have never since kissed a man in that same way and with the same meaning again. I was a young girl who had a bigger crush than most on Bobby Sherman. He always asked me to kiss him and I believe he liked it.

Ethel C. Richard

*What is a love song
without the kiss?*

*We were the dance and
the song for a moment.
And the sweet melody still lives
within the mist of yesterday.*

*Never having slept it is
alive with eternal movement.*

*Never having to be quelled it simply breathes
within each beat of my heart.*

*Let's suffice to say
I loved the kisses.*

*Roses have the most beautiful scent
in the world from a flower.*

*Ethel as a teen believed
that the most wonderful scent
in the world from a man*

*Was the close up scent
of Bobby Sherman's earlobe!*

I would have faced anything to be near Bobby… even the frightening things of the road were not enough to keep me away…I would have walked through fire just to brush my lips upon his face again…I was that totally devoted.

The Bobby Sherman Miracle

My Early Years
(Birth to Fourteen)

Where do I take you my reader from here? Where did this story really begin?

Mom and Dad met at Dads brother's apartment when Mom was visiting with Irene (Dad's brother Raymond's wife) who was Mom's friend. Dad liked her and asked his brother to ask his wife to ask my Mom if she would agree to go to a movie with him the following week. Mom said yes and while at the movie Dad asked Mom, "want to get married?" They were married the following Tuesday on September 7, 1954. Mom always said that they'd met two weeks before they got married. Their marriage was bereft with difficulties though. Dad drank alcohol and smoked and Mom hated alcohol and cigarettes.

Both had been married before and Mom was a widow and Dad was divorced. Having been previously married in the Catholic faith by the diocese Dad was unable to get an annulment from the church to marry my mother (especially her being a Baptist) so they married at the JP's office downtown.

This always bothered Dad because as he'd say, "My life is messed up and I can't get around this thing that I somehow have two wives".

One day when Dad was standing in front of the police chief at the Manchester Station (Mom had filed a complaint with them that Dad was not supporting us kids properly) and the Police Chief told Dad to empty his pockets and I was

Ethel C. Richard

there and saw and heard the whole thing.

Dad emptied his pockets and put his wallet and stuff up on the counter. The Officer said to him 'YOUR WIFE TELLS ME THAT YOU HAVE NOT BEEN SUPPORTING YOUR FAMILY"…Dad replied in surprise, "which wife? I have two!"

"That's bigamy in these parts!" the Chief answered back.

To this day I laugh at the scene in my memory. The church had really messed up my Dad's thinking.

It made me very sensitive and thoughtful though of person's emotional problems and very interested in psychology and religion in my young years. I was seven years old when Mom brought me and Eddie with her to make complaints at the Police Department against Dad. Let's fill you in on me personally. We'll start at the beginning with as much as I can now remember. I was one year old and crawling around in the kitchen behind the stove when I eyed a small can of range oil on the floor and thought I would have a drink.

I was carried to the hospital while I was falling asleep. That's all I remember about it (honest). Let's go to a toddler about one and a half years old trying to sleep while on her knees and elbows in her crib rocking back and forth. I had another accident while playing in the kitchen. Mom had been boiling water in the electric skillet and I reached up and pulled it down on top of myself. Mom tried to help. She pulled my shirt off fast and I completely lost the skin that had been on my chest. The doctor at the hospital said that mine were third degree burns. He had wrapped me in Vaseline and bandages and sent me home.

The Bobby Sherman Miracle

After some amount of time a stench became apparent and Mom insisted to dad that I go back to the hospital. The doctor kept me there in a cast of some kind for three months while they also treated me for wet gangrene. For months I could not sleep in a normal position but had to sleep on my knees and elbows. I actually remember rocking. I was very uncomfortable.

At five a number of things happened. The things I remember with most clarity are these.

I am not sure when it started but I would go to bed every night and pray like crazy and cry a lot. I would pray about things that I am sure kids should not be even thinking about.

As young as four and five I had such a huge internal agony of thoughts. I guess I thought that there had to be an important reason why I was alive. I begged god that my life could be used by him to help many people so that they can come to heaven. I told him that I did not want for my life to be all for nothing.

I told him that I did not believe that anyone loved me. I told him that I was alone and could not get a hug or a kiss. I asked god, "Do you love me…? Can you help me ….? I want a hug too, like other kids, and I do not want other people to hurt like I do" and I would recite the Jesus Loves Me song quietly or the Our Father prayer in whispers as I cried.

I prayed for my parents and others very faithfully every night for years and I also silently prayed throughout each day. I had learned to do that from the New Testament.

1 Thessalonians 5:17 says, "Pray incessantly."

When I was a kid sometimes I would hurt so bad that I felt an awful physical ache inside and would hold onto myself and tell myself that everything will be alright. That I would someday feel better. I never once thought to wish to die. I always wanted to live so that my life would not become good for nothing.

The Our Father Prayer (The Lord's Prayer) Matthew 6: 9-13 - After this manner therefore pray ye: Our Father which art in heaven, Hallowed be thy name. Thy kingdom come. Thy will be done in earth, as it is in heaven. Give us this day our daily bread. And forgive us our debts, as we forgive our debtors. And lead us not into temptation, but deliver us from evil: for thine is the kingdom, and the power, and the glory, forever. Amen.

One day I was playing at my friend Linda's apartment which was the next door down from ours on the porch. (Our apartments were on the top floor). While in the kitchen with Linda's seventeen year old brother David I saw my dad's watch up on the shelf and I got upset because I knew that he had stolen the watch from my house. I got so angry that I told him I was going to tell my dad he'd stolen his watch.

David chased me all over his apartment until he finally cornered me into the dark closet and he locked me in and would not let me out. I do not remember exactly how I got out. Still I do remember how scary it was. My dad did find out about his watch because I told him later what David had done and he got his watch back again.

Sometime later during the winter David was sitting in the back seat of my dad's car with me while my mom and dad were in the front seat and he touched me in a wrong place and told me not to tell. I want to be open in this report and so I have just divulged a secret previously never known. It would be good if parents kept a closer eye on their children so that such things would never happen to them.

During the following spring I and my brother Eddie who was three years old were playing in the kitchen and my mom was gone somewhere. I think she'd gone to the drug store down the street. My dad was at the gas range and frying up some potatoes. He had a can of lard and had just put some into the pan.

There was a window above the stove which had a large green shade hanging to the sill the entire length of the window which began just above the burners by about eight inches.

Suddenly the grease in the pan caught fire and the fire leaped into the air and caught the shade which burst into bright orange flames. I stood there and saw my dad quickly climb onto the stove and struggling to battle the fire with his bare hands. The fire reached the ceiling and dad yelled at me and Eddie, "You kids get out of the house!"

I had watched as Eddie ran into the bedroom and climb under the bed. I listened to my dad and I ran into the bedroom and went under the bed with Eddie and he asked me in a really scared voice, "Is it over yet?"

"Eddie, we have to go," I answered. "Come on! Come with me!" I grabbed his hand and brought him through the door and out through the kitchen to the porch.

We stood there on the porch while Dad kept working on the fire which had burned a large part of the ceiling over the stove. I don't remember exactly what happened after that except that Dad had burned his hands and his scalp pretty badly and went to the hospital. My dad had been a volunteer

Ethel C. Richard

fireman in those days when he was younger.

We had to move out of that apartment after the fire.

We moved into another apartment within the same building but on a different floor and to make things worse there were "firebugs" in the building and in the surrounding area. Dad was always with an eye out for kids holding gasoline cans. It was scary living there. We were very poor and so I had to sleep in my crib till I was six years old and then my dad got me a big metal "grownup" bed.

Dad seemed to get upset with mom a lot. Mom was Baptist and Dad was catholic as was I.

Dad at night would sometimes talk rough with Mom after they went to bed. I would get scared and holler out in the night, "Daddy, please! Don't hurt Mommy!"

He would yell back, "Go to sleep!"

He drank beer down at the club and sometimes they would get in an argument because mom hated alcohol and did not always want to kiss him. He got frustrated and would go out and visit his ex wife and mom would dress us up at 11 pm and even at two in the morning to bring us walking with her to his ex wife's apartment to go find him and chastise him verbally for not coming home.

I was so exhausted walking in the street with mom and three year old Eddie when we made that trip that I immediately fell asleep on the floor when we got inside while listening to my dad raise his voice at mom for having dragged us down the street to her place.

It was a tough life being a kid at our home.

After we moved from the building where the fire took

place we moved around every year from one apartment to another. Don't get me wrong. Dad worked for 30 years for the same shoe factory. He was not a loafer. He could be very helpful when he wanted to be.

When there was a fight on a holiday within the extended family he would always step in to break it up. He had a reputation for being the nice guy in the family. He was the guy who would yell at you but lend to you money or cigarettes or provide the transport that you begged him for when you just had to go someplace. He was Union Steward for the workers at his place of work and the people there loved him.

Many, many people showed up to pay respect at his wake and we had no idea who all the many people were and there had been a few hundred. In his later years Dad quit drinking and went on long walks with Mom, watched baseball on TV and liked to take Mom out to a BINGO game once a week.

Mom was very straight laced. Refused to drink anything but ginger ale at a party and was against gambling, smoking and any drug stronger than an aspirin. Dad taught me to play poker and gave me cigarettes when I turned 14 (and he put a whiskey highball in my hand after I got out of the hospital at around 17 years old). I had not been allowed alcohol at home until that day and I was not big on drinking and so I did not finish it. I liked to drink coffee and a little tea or a soda. I smoked cigarettes as did Dad. Looking back at my early childhood I can understand that I was very insecure. Mom and dad were not terribly open with affection and I do not remember that me or Eddie ever got a hug or a kiss.

I could give to my dad a small kiss on the forehead once a

Ethel C. Richard

year at Christmas or at New Year's Eve. Father's Day or on Mother's Day I could kiss mom. Easter was ok for that too. The rest of the year we had a family ritual which I do not know where it came from but here is how it go's...

"Dad, shake hands? We're pals, ok?"

"Good night, sleep tight and don't let the bedbugs bite!"

I and Eddie would take turns with Dad in this ritual every night. I would get to the actual shaking hands part with Mom and every night she'd try to trick me and I would be afraid of the hand shake.

Note: whenever Mom got really upset with me she told me, "You're dad's favorite... but you've always been the black sheep of the family...." (maybe because I chose Catholicism and poker and cigarettes?)

I still shake my head over this one...!

When it was my turn to shake hands with mom she'd shake my hand out and tell me to relax and then she'd yank hard and really pull me off balance and it upset me. To really bring on the apprehension was the fact that we did as kids have bugs in our beds. Ugh... I HATED THE WHOLE THING.

I WOULD TRY AND BE VERY CAREFUL TO AVOID THE BEDBUGS and so I didn't get much sleep.

WAS TERRIFIED TO SLEEP IN MY BED. When I was 14 just before the real trouble started in my neighborhood I woke up one morning with my torso being covered about a half inch deep with black fleas and I screamed holy hell and jumped up and down trying to shake them all off of me and swearing the whole time at my parents.

I stormed out of the apartment yelling my head off in

total anger swearing that I was NEVER coming back once I escaped that hell hole. There had been another time when I was younger when I woke up screaming because a rat had cuddled up to my neck while I was sleeping. My mom came in and tore my clothes off. The rat ran and I was pretty shook up too! I always seemed to put my fingers in wrong places and so I many times made trips to the hospital with broken fingers. The car door frame was apparently not something I could understand as a dangerous spot to park my hand.

Every finger has been broken except my thumbs. Another time Mom had been sewing and our loved dog Blacky got hold of the needle and went totally mad and ran the walls in a circle of our living room as he was dying. I freaked out and couldn't stop crying because Blacky was killed by the needle and dragged out by the neck on a loop by the catcher man who came and looped him and took him away. I yelled at the man for killing our dog. It was not the man's fault. But I was nine when it happened and I could not handle watching Blacky crying and running and completely losing all control of himself and then being dragged out of our apartment on a stick. I felt like I had died that day.

It's not that mom was a bad mother... she would get distracted (and who would believe that the dog will eat a needle)?...and I was an inquisitive and daring little person too who would be prone as a habit to get into mischief. Mom chased me once in awhile with a tree branch or a broom... She NEVER landed them though (I was too fast on my feet)!

Hear me now. It was not totally bad days all of the time. Sometimes we got to eat American cheese. (I love cheese and usually never got any because it's expensive).

Ethel C. Richard

We occasionally went out for ice cream or to a drive-in movie or went to the lake to have a cookout and swim. On Palm Sunday I got palm leaves and on Easter Mom got a lily and we kids opened Easter baskets. We got new clothes. We had a nice dinner. Dad wanted to see us happy on holidays…all holidays. I have learned to forgive Mom and Dad all of their shortcomings and in later years while Mom was dying I took care of her and I gave her many warm hugs to let her know that I love her.

We had affection toward the end of her life and I am grateful for that change and I consider it a blessing. I forgive people when I know it is right to do so. Some people do evil as a habit and with no remorse and it is a mistake to forgive evil. Some people simply make serious mistakes and learn from them and they deserve a hand up and a chance to show that they have changed and will better themselves. After all everyone grows at a different pace.

You see through the window of my eyes as I was when a child when you read these words and it's my hope that in my regurgitating this stuff that was, that I can somehow help some other poor and lonely and pained kid through the seriously rough times in life. I was then and continue to be the enemy of suicide. I fight with all my power for life and for the absolute happiest and productive charitable life possible to obtain. Good health and quality in strength of character and strong families are worth pursuing and each individual has a right to achieve personal betterment and true happiness.

In the next chapter we can ditch the negative stuff we saw here and visit a place more up-lifting.

Chapter Three

Sister M. St. Phil'eas

If ever I loved a lady it was my fifth grade catechism teacher. She was short, stout and about 70 years old. She wore a full habit and she was stunning in her beads. She was also the greatest and most patent and kindest teacher of prayers I had ever encountered. I came to my own under her instruction.

It was because of her belief in me that I was able to climb mountains emotionally and educationally while I attended her classes. I was very religious and she used that to help me learn my lessons. I loved my prayer book that she had given me (even taking it to bed with me and kissing my rosary cross).

My Catechism prayers book was loaded with many

Ethel C. Richard

wonderful prayers and invocations. I memorized my favorites and became a devout worshiper, even considering joining the convent. I was eleven years old and we lived less than a block from Sacred Heart Grade School. It was while in Sacred Heart Parish that me and Eddie had first communion. I lived to go to mass. I attended mass on Sundays and many times during the week.

I studied hard in my classes and I did extra studies in spelling and science. I loved reading geography, social studies and travel books I became interested in psychiatry and psychology and arts such as sculpting, architecture, photography and painting. I took voice lessons to learn how to control my breathing while in vocals for solo and chorus.

I began studying theater arts and listened to many types of music. I especially loved musicals such as My Fair Lady, Carousel and The Sound of Music. I sometimes listened to Mahalia Jackson and Cowboy Copas. I liked Shakespeare. I had a library of his works). I became interested in dance and yoga movement incorporated in dance. I started writing poetry, prose and sonnets.

In my spare time I also put together model PT boats and it was really fun to construct all those little aircraft. (I was a little bit of a tomboy and I liked shooting with my brothers toy Johnny 007 military power gun. It was like 10 guns rolled into one good sized machine gun). I was also a baseball player though not very good at it. It's hard to hit the ball when you can't really see it coming!

I got involved with the spelling bee competition in school. I really loved trying to figure out the tricks involved in

The Bobby Sherman Miracle

making the varying sounds of the letters in words.

I came to realize that if you knew the patterns in formation of English words that you could understand the spelling of a word just by carefully listening to its pronunciation. I analyzed every sound in the words and learned semantics, and that's why I am very careful to follow the philosophy to "mean what you say and to say what you mean."

To do the opposite is to invite misunderstanding. Lots of folks who know me think I am very boring at times because for fun I will look up words in the dictionary and study their various meanings.

I analyze what persons say on a daily basis. It's such a habit with me and that's probably because it was more than just a hobby with me when I was involved with the spelling bee competitions. It paid off for a little while back then. I was chosen to represent the entire fifth grade parochial school population of New Hampshire in the National Competitions. Regrettably, I was not able to compete at that level because my parents were not in agreement with the school to allow me to travel to Washington, D.C. (even with a chaperone) in order to participate. Our school Dean was forced to send my runner up (Irene Cedras) instead.

I don't think that it's necessary here to go into exactly how upset I was at the realization that I was being denied my place at the nationals because of my parents inability to understand its importance to my future. If I'd won the competition I would have had a very nice scholarship.

After all, I loved to study and to learn. That and my religion was my whole life.

Ethel C. Richard

I had written a letter to The University of Warwick in Coventry, England and told the officers of the coed theater program there about my successes in school and about how I was the top student of the fifth grade for parochial schools and chosen as winner of the bees from New Hampshire during 1966 to participate at Washington, DC in the national bees. I told them about my interest in theater and Shakespeare and how I would love to study theater at their university because Shakespeare from the age of about 16 had worked with theater troupes that performed at St. Mary's Guildhall in Coventry.

The university officers had responded to my inquiry with an acceptance letter and information about the school program and the campus. I was so excited to have been accepted but when my parents found out about my acceptance by the university they shot that down as well and for the same reasons.

I felt like the rug had been pulled out from beneath me and my future was done and so I hated my favorite dictionary for quite a while afterward. Still, Sacred Heart Parish, Sacred Heart School, My catechism teacher Sister. St. Phil'eas, my english teacher Lorraine Loiselle and my winning the bee will always remain in my heart as my favorite memory of childhood.

My family soon had to move to the east side of the city and our parish changed too. I was admitted into Our Lady of Perpetual Help School in East Manchester and things had changed quite a bit for me there. It was while I attended school there that Mom got sick and had to go to the hospital

The Bobby Sherman Miracle

to have surgery. She was gone for maybe three weeks.

I had a lot of time on my hands as Dad worked all day and I was basically alone to do what I wanted. It was during that year when I first got a glimpse of Bobby Sherman as an actor in Here Come the Brides.

I liked the show and like other Brides fans I enjoyed the character he played on the show. I was around thirteen years old then and it was at that time in my life when I started reading teen celebrity magazines like 16 and Tiger Beat. My taste in music expanded to include The Beatles, Donovan, Melanie, Grand Funk Railroad, Joplin, The Grass Roots, Moody Blues, Steppenwolf, Three Dog Night and Billy Preston.

Though I thought Bobby had a great voice I was not into his style of music and I had only one Bobby Album.

We were poor at my home anyway and I only had a small record collection and was very particular in my tastes. I got my one Bobby Sherman album, "Bobby Sherman" from Columbia Record House in a .99 cent deal (14 free records when you agree to buy three a year at regular price).

Like I already said, I wanted to meet him but it was because to me he seemed to have a good head on his shoulders and good moral character and he was interested in many of the same things I was, like psychology and photography.

I also liked looking at him. I felt a strong physical attraction when I looked at his photos. I liked the articles about him in the magazines. He seemed like he could make a great family man and could be a good choice for marriage and make a good dad for his kids. So I was

Ethel C. Richard

interested in Bobby as a person and not particularly for the bubble gum music that he performed.

Let's jump ahead about six months to the summer of 1969.

I was into screaming blue meanies and Peter Max. I wore a Max belt buckle and I played guitar. I wrote tunes. I was dabbling in both six string and base. I was teaching myself rifts. When I was fourteen, The Grass Roots Group came to Manchester Armory Auditorium for the Manchester Summer Series Concerts that the city sponsored that year. Elvin Bishop Group was the band appearing with them on the bill.

I went to the concert as a Rob Grill fan (Lead singer of The Grassroots) and I ended up leaving the auditorium with Perry Welsh who was singing lead with Elvin Bishop Group.

He'd approached me while I was in front of the stage between sets. I said to him, "Do you always try to pick up girls at your concerts?"

He replied, "Only the good looking ones!"

I was flattered by it and I liked his vocals so I went along with him to their hotel.

There were other girls who were picked up by the other few band members too but they kind of flipped out after arriving at the hotel room. I mean to say that the other girls behaved like they were goody two shoes and couldn't even communicate on what I thought was any real level of maturity.

After all we'd all agreed to come along and it did not appear that the guys were dangerous and it was not like we'd been invited there to be raped.

The guys basically just wanted some company and compared to many men the band members that night behaved

The Bobby Sherman Miracle

like gentlemen. They kept hands off if contact was not wanted.

They asked the other girls what was the problem with sitting with them within their hotel room on the bed to talk and maybe have a beer or a soda. But the girls were uncomfortable with it and left. They criticized the guys and I had to wonder why they'd even come along in the first place!

They were acting scared like it was all just about sex for the guys. They were a bummer to the guys and to me as well because I in no way felt threatened and I did not understand their animosity as absolutely nothing had happened of a negative nature and yet the other girls were very highly judgmental.

I and Perry just lay around and talked for a few hours while he had a beer. There was no sex. He was not pushy at all and he was very nice. He asked me to come with the band to New York and so I guess he was interested in me. I liked him but I could not justify doing that to my family.

The way I saw it, I would have to suddenly disappear and make a phone call to my parents that I was in New York with a band who was on a nationwide tour. It would have devastated my mom and so I told him in the early morning just after dawn that I could not go with them and that I had better go home.

I told him that if he wanted to he could write to me. He didn't write and so I forgot about it and I let it go. The contrast is striking in my attitude toward leaving my family at that time compared to my indifferent attitude toward my family AFTER I'd been involuntarily committed to the State Hospital and placed on their "therapeutic" program of

Ethel C. Richard

Thorazine drug cocktails and electric shock.

Now back to my story about the prior year before I turned fourteen...

I continued to play baseball with my friends and I liked to hang out in my back yard with the trees and lawn. I love nature and it was natural for me to quietly sit in a garden and just think and watch grasshoppers and feel the warm breezes of summer. I liked to dig up earthworms and go fishing with my brother. I rode a bike like every kid and I went snow sledding in the winter. Remember the wood sleds with metal blades? I loved sledding and we always had a ball going down the slopes. There was a way to steer the sled for best speed and it was great for rise in adrenalin.

It could be dangerous sometimes though and I found out how the hard way how tricky it could be to approach any other kid who'd had the unfortunate experience to wipe out with one and get injured. I and Eddie were out sledding in back of the house from up on a four foot wall that had been embanked by hard packed snow. There was a thick pipe we did not see sticking up out of the pavement just before the top of the wall before the slope by about ten inches. (It had been covered). Eddie crashed head on into it and split his head open. I ran to him and asked him if he were ok. He just picked up another pipe and hit me hard directly over the head.

So now we both had an injury and I got the point. I ran up the stairs to get Mom and we all went to the hospital and me and Eddie needed stitches. Eddie says it did not happen this way and that he was the only one who needed the stitches. So, in my report I have to give him equal time in the interest of fairness in disagreement. I believe I still have the scar to prove he hit me over the head….!

Where were we in this story anyway?

Yes. O. L. P. H. Sixth grade….

What a contrast I can draw between the two schools of Sacred Heart and O. L. P. H.

O. L. P. H. was a disaster in my life.

The nuns were nasty and treacherous and if you made it out of that school with your fingers not having been broken by a metal ruler you'd have been very lucky.

The mother superior who ran the school was my enemy. Plain and simply she hated me. I did lousy in French class and she tore up my precious indulgence that the good Father had given to me right in front of me , the class and the priest, telling everyone there that I was not deserving to receive the gift.

I wanted to get Sister M. St. Phil'eas and my former dean to come and kick her ass!

She'd looked inside my small clutch and found a small tube of pink lipstick (that my Mom had given to me) and a cigarette.

She literally dragged me into her office and sitting with two other nuns she asked me, "Do you want and enjoy being a tramp?" She did not like my response (which was literally no response) and so she expelled me from the school. I was

Ethel C. Richard

then sent to Southside Middle School for a short time and then moved again from Southside to Maynard School and then to Parkside Middle School in West Manchester.

We now lived on Fourth Street and it was a big, huge mistake. This neighborhood was heavy gang territory and we were now living in Hell zone. There was full heavy gang activity literally at our front door.

We were directly across the street from the park and it is a very narrow street. I believe I will publish a photo of the street location where we lived so that everyone reading this can understand the serious dangers there at that time. But before I get too far ahead of myself I want to backtrack and talk about an event that happened to me and was very significant in my life that did influence me in the following few years.

I hope my readers are not squeamish because this story is difficult to deal with when it's realized that this kind of thing actually happens sometimes to persons even here in the states.

I am writing about it because parents must be informed why it is so important to protect your kids and know what is happening with them at all times.

I am not saying to be overly protective of your children but you need to be aware of what is happening in your neighborhoods and what persons live there who may be a threat to your families.

I had been walking in the street in broad daylight and holding a cigarette in my fingers when I was attacked (being a girl smoking the cigarette was the reason my attackers did what they did) because of their poor upbringing and twisted religious opinion.

The Bobby Sherman Miracle

I tried to do what my Mom had taught me which was to just keep walking if you are harassed while in the streets. The rock was as big as a large mans fist. It was very jagged being pavement tar. I say rock because it hit me so hard that I momentarily lost consciousness. I saw another rock next to it later on the ground where it happened. It's possible I was hit more than once. I did hear the kid yell to his friend, "Let's stone her!" So there had been more than one person involved.

I had been hit on the left side of my head on the temple and the face and there was blood falling into my throat and choking me. My mouth was all torn up inside of my cheeks and I was extremely disoriented, struggling to stand and to walk. I focused on trying to get to my aunts home which was not far. I did get there and when my aunt saw me she pulled me inside quickly and spent quite some time stopping the bleeding and packing my nose. I do not remember if I was brought to the hospital. Like I said, I was very shook up, scared and disoriented. Ok, enough of that.

After O. L. P. H. I was sent to South Side and shortly later transferred to Maynard School, which was a public school. Our family also moved again.

I became friends with Andrena who had moved to Manchester from Scotland with her family. Her father was a minister. Andrena Carslaw was an angel of a girl and a great friend. She taught me the Scottish Highlander Dance. I am part Scot (Mom's side of the family) and so I really enjoyed that. We went to school together and were in the same class.

Chapter Four

On Moving Too Much, Mr. Petrick and We Clowns,
The Neighborhood Referral Office (and)
Eddie Has an Accident

Mr. Petrick was one of the best teachers around. Give credit where credit is due. He had real intelligence and knew how to get best performance out of his students. Since we were a somewhat immature bunch he nicknamed us all clowns and meted out many a stiff penalty when we got out of line. I loved Mr. Petrick's way. He rocked on his heels as he spoke to the class. I only got into trouble with him one time. He told me to write 500 times on a paper that, "I will not talk in class".

It worked for me...! I got straight A's while at Maynard School. My very best subject was science. There was nothing too unusual about that because I was a female kid Einstein. I was crazy about physics and astronomy and photo-genesis. My bag was also in archeology… more specifically Biblical

Ethel C. Richard

Archeology.

Still more important than this, I was becoming interested in school again. Mom had gotten better over the course of several months and she was now at home looking after my small brother Donald. I was thirteen and Don was three.

I started getting interested in social service work and so I began visiting almost daily with some people who worked in the neighborhood social services referral agency. They were very nice and welcomed me as a friend and talked with me about themselves and their occupation.

Eddie Carr was one of my best friends. Eddie was about thirty years old and married with kids. He was very friendly and helpful and never judgmental when we were discussing various subjects and it did not matter whether we talked politics or religion. He was always obliging of a good debate and an all-around fun person to talk with. His wife was just as nice as he was and she'd often be around for a smile.

My friend Andrena had to move back to Scotland after a few months and my friends at the referral office were so nice to hang with that I went to visit with them often.

My Dad did not like me to visit there. He did not like it that I was hanging around with adults. Though my teachers liked my novels and my singing and invited me to take part in shows at school, dad did not like the novels I wrote or the lyrics I'd duplicated from current pop songs. Dad was upset that the content of the material was too adult and he later brought all of my writings and lyrics to the psychiatrist and he told the psychiatrist that I was writing promiscuous stories. He accused me of writing the lyrics to Dusty Springfield's hit

The Bobby Sherman Miracle

song, "Son of a Preacher Man." Believe me it really was this stupid and I was really committed to the hospital based on this bogus stuff!

Let's change the subject.

I was with Mom and Donald one afternoon when there came a frantic knock at our door. Eddie had been hit by a car in the alley behind the house while riding his bike. Mom told me to stay with Don while she ran out the door. I grabbed Donald and ran out behind her. Eddie was lying sprawled out unconscious stomach down on the street and had tire marks on his back. I and Mom were scared to death worried. He was taken to the hospital by ambulance and Mom went with him.

Later that day Mom and Dad came home together and told me that Eddie had a concussion and would be in the hospital for a couple of weeks but that he would be ok. The hospital would not allow me and Don to visit so we had to wait to see him until after he got back home. We moved again after he got out of the hospital. We were at that apartment for only a few months and then we moved once again.

Enter Into "Hell Hole"

Living at Hell Hole in West Manchester, N.H. in 1969 turned out to be the most wretched nightmare of my life. At first it was not so bad. I got to visit with my aunt Madeline Gabert who lived upstairs in the old Granite Square block. We used to have fun private girl talks while sitting in her kitchen. I was not hanging with the kids that would gather at the park across the street from our building.

Ethel C. Richard

I went to school and I only had one girlfriend. I would sometimes walk to her house and pick her up and go walking to the store with her or hang with her at her house. I turned fourteen in June and without much event.

After school was out for summer vacation things started going badly in the neighborhood. The kids in the park were often being talked about as being trouble makers. I heard that some old folks were being badgered and bullied and their money and groceries stolen from them when they came out of the grocery store next to the square on the other side of the park as they exited the store.

Photo of the Barr & Clapp Building (Old Granite Square) in West Manchester near to the park where Ethel was attacked and from where her escape at 15 years old took place appears courtesy of the Manchester, New Hampshire Historical Association.

Many of the kids that hung out together at the park were kids that were in my classes at school. There were young adults

The Bobby Sherman Miracle

on motor cycles also hanging around and talking with the kids and there was money and drugs and alcohol being floated. It was obvious that there were some none too clean deals being made in the park. I was not allowed to go into the park at night.

When school came around in September I ran into a problem with some people. There was a group of girls standing together outside of the school grounds that started to bully me as I walked passed (they shoved me and knocked me down and my books went flying to the ground) and I got really mad at the front person and I kicked her in the stomach when she came at me again.

She fell backward onto her butt and then all of the kids backed off. Suddenly the same kids were at my side and I said nothing and walked away. Eddie was there and saw what happened and he asked me if I was alright. We walked home together.

After that small altercation all of the popular kids in my class wanted to be my friend.

It was a strange twist of events that some of the kids who hung out at the park were in my class. Groups of girls came to my home and starting knocking on my door. I just kind of shook my head and went with it. It was a way of not being bullied that is too strange and after what happened later I certainly would not ever recommend this method of protection.

You see, I had inadvertently become too chummy with the very group that was causing the trouble at the Park.

I HAD NOT MEANT TO EARN THE "RESPECT" OF THE GANG RELATIVE KIDS (related into the gang

Ethel C. Richard

families) but it seemed it was the twisted circumstance of my life that crazy situations seem to drop into my lap.

I did not want trouble and so I avoided too loud or crazy behavior people. I was not a party goer and I was a quiet person and so I really was a loner because I avoided other kids except for my brothers.

I went to only one party (did not know it was a gang member's parent's house) making a mistake because I did not know the family... and at that lousy event I met a certain boy I still wish I'd never met and I truthfully wish I'd never gone to the party.

When we got there the adults were serving around beer to everyone (including the teenagers). There were both adults and kids all doing the same things. There were people in every room and mostly very rough and shameless people. You know that oldies song, "Mama told me not to come"? That's exactly how I felt. I went outside on the porch and I had a cigarette with a boy who had struck up a conversation with me inside.

We talked a while and then he asked me if I wanted to go for a walk. We left together and we walked to a place down near the river. We were all alone and it was dark and he told me while we were standing on the rocks that he and some other boy had killed another kid. I then became very fearful but I did not let on because I knew he could not be very stable mentally.

I was very nice to him and I really did not respond to what he'd said except to nod my head slightly and grabbed his hand showing some compassion. (I knew enough to hide my fear in such a circumstance).

I quietly and sweetly walked away from the rocks (we were standing on a huge rock surrounded with river water when it suddenly occurred to me that I was talking with a killer at 10:30 pm in near pitch dark at the end of an isolated path and standing on a rock that all the kids in the neighborhood called "The Bucket" (where some people would have drinking parties) that sits directly on the river. It was NOT a place to be with a homicidal maniac... not that any place is a good place to be with a homicidal maniac!

So I became very conscious of what he'd said while trying to convince him that I was a friend. I kissed him and held his hand and I told him after a few minutes that it was getting late and that we should go home. I gave him a hug and we walked holding hands the quarter mile or so back into the street area. I felt strongly that I had to pretend that I liked him. We had been down a dark path and into the woods under the trestle where the river meets the shore on the rocks.

Later that night I was very relieved to be back inside my bedroom and not anywhere near him.

Over the following week I'd made phone calls to try and report the details that he had confessed to me to the local police department. The officers I spoke with were not helpful. They kept telling me that they could not investigate without having the identity of who was killed. I got angry at the police because they would not believe me. I did not return to the park for several days. However on the following weekend I had to walk to the store to get some things.

It was about eight pm and as I crossed the street to enter the store the boy pulled up in a vehicle. He was driving and he had two or three boys from the gang with him in the car. It was raining as he pulled the car up beside me and with the window rolled fully down he asked me to get into the car with them. I could smell beer on his breath and I bent over slightly and looked him directly in the eye and told him, "you are drinking, it's raining and I am not going with you."

He died that night and the boys with him in the car were sent to the hospital in critical condition. He'd told the others who hung out at the park that I was his girlfriend. (We'd only been together that one time the night of the party). My parents would not allow me to go to his funeral and forced me to stay behind at class while the school had allowed all of the other kids who knew him to attend his funeral.

The kids that went to his funeral were very angry with me because I did not attend and blamed me for his death saying that if I'd gone with him that he would not have crashed the car. They said that he was upset because his girlfriend refused to go with him that night and so he crashed his car. I knew that he was out to destroy himself and everyone involved in the crime he and they had committed or who knew of what they'd done. I knew it that rainy night that to get into his car would mean death and that's why I'd refused.

The Bobby Sherman Miracle

The attitude of the neighborhood gang of kids turned hostile toward me and they started coming to my house to harass me. They threw rocks at our windows and demanded of my Mom that I come outside.

I became upset to go to school and I refused to go. Then one day I finally walked into the Hillside Middle School principal's office (Mr. Campbell) and put both my hands palms down onto his desk and leaning into him and threateningly looking him directly in the eye I "ordered" him to expel me immediately from his school or that I would walk out anyway.

He told me that we could work out a compromise. He arranged a half day schedule for me (which worked because I did not want to run into the gang members every time I left school at two pm). Unfortunately the principal was thrown by my behavior since he did not understand what was happening after school and he arranged for me to see a psychologist.

That's how I got thrown into the state psychiatric system. They started me with appointments at the local mental health center and I was told to go there every Tuesday for counseling. It was around the same time when I met Jack (Morin) and we became friends. I'll explain more about Jack a bit later on. He stayed in our cellar for a couple of weeks, and then he got his own place after getting enough money from his new job. His place was on the east side of the city and so I walked over to hang out with him instead of hanging around my building and the park. After the trouble started I started staying out a lot and even sneaking out when my folks were not looking.

Ethel C. Richard

The hospital record on one page has it that I ran away from home three times (and not two) but I had not remembered running away three times. It was only after I began to realize that certain facts in the documents did not line up with what I did have for memory when I discovered that an entire set of documents from Burbank police and the Superior Court of Los Angeles had been misplaced.

What finally tipped me off and proved to me that there had actually been a third trip I'd made from Manchester to Burbank that summer was the address listed in paperwork from the court of my parents address.

You see...my folks had moved from Fourth Street while I was missing and on the road. Here is where my detective work had to dig up the truth because I was returned to my folks home (which was still at 81 Fourth Street) by the Los Angeles Courts who'd bought my plane ticket back to Manchester the first time I'd been taken into custody in Burbank. I remember having a huge upset while on the way to my folks place in dad's car. Dad had yelled at me and told me to "shut up!" when I was telling him and mom about Bobby and my friends in Burbank. I'd sworn because of that before even getting out of his car that I did not belong with him and mom in Manchester and that I would be back at Bobby's side within the week. I left the following afternoon... and I'd left from Fourth Street. All of the Burbank police and Superior Court papers that I have list the Lake Avenue address and with different dates entirely for having been taken into custody in Burbank. So the hospital record is correct. I'd gone to Burbank three times and not two as I'd originally supposed.

Now again let's change the subject....

I know that at 14 years old (just before I'd been hospitalized for the first time) I'd been approached by my father's brother Raymond for sex just before Christmas that year - which totally pissed me off (and I was not feeling too trusting or charitable after that... and so I did not stay home much). Dad did not listen to me when I explained to him what his brother had done and Dad only got very angry with me, accusing me of a lie.

Chapter Five

Family Betrayal, Abandonment & Dr. Kutras

Well, Dad did it. Dad went berserk because I'd complained against his brother and because I'd stayed out all night. He brought all of my writings and lyrics and a letter or two to a psychiatrist and told the guy that I was making up stories and had been staying out all night, talking about sex, hanging with older people (some of them men) swearing and seriously wreaking havoc.

I do not remember my first counselor's name. Kutras however I do remember with great dismay. I met him only once and that was the day I told him to shove his pills. He sat there and told me that he'd gotten reports about me that my behavior was not so good. It was the way he looked down at me with his eyes wide that made me want to spit.

I got sarcastic and I told him, "Let's just say that I am

Ethel C. Richard

psychic and I can read your mind. I do not need those pills, ok. You can keep your pills and shove them!" After I got home from his office there came a phone call for my father. I picked up the extension quietly and listened in as Kutras told my father that I was very seriously mentally ill and would require hospitalization.

He said that he was sending a social worker to the house within an hour to help him bring me to the State Hospital in Concord and sign me in as an inpatient.

I was completely floored at what was happening and I put the phone down, took my cigarettes and some money and went to the pizza place down the street trying to think.

I was pretty distraught and scared and I was hoping they would give up on it. I was there for maybe an hour or so when the social worker walked into the restaurant and sat down in my booth.

Her name was Gloria and she'd brought me a book of poems by Rod McKuen. She was trying to coax me into getting into the car and Dad must have told her that I like poetry.

She sat there trying to cheer me up and telling me that the hospital was not a bad place and that kids go to movies or swimming and can listen to music and go to school there etc.... ad nauseam. Then she told me that I had to go to the hospital because there was a court order.

The Bobby Sherman Miracle

```
PROGRESS NOTES    All notes to be signed by person making note, and Attending Physician
```

1/21/70

CONVALESCENT STATUS SUMMARY (as of 4/17/70)

This is the first admission for this fourteen year old white, single Catholic girl who was admitted to the New Hampshire Hospital on 1/21/70 on a Regular Order of Commitment signed by Drs. Rene Lambert and Robert A. Dammaraia. She was brought to the New Hampshire Hospital from her home in Manchester, New Hampshire by her father and the State Welfare Worker.

The commitment paper reads as follows: "The patient said, "I want to go to England and become an actress. I have psychic power. I am too old for my age. They don't understand me. The worse thing in my life has been to grow up. I have slight problem with my nerves. Laughing in an exaggerated manner. Her hair was not combed. Her thinking was fragmented, poor and unrealistic. She has been having problems in school. She has not been taking her medication as prescribed. There were some loosening of associations and feelings of rejection."

DIAGNOSIS: Acute schizophrenic episode.

MANIFESTATIONS: Manic behavior, pressure of speech, flightive ideas, inability to achieve in school and unmanageability at home.

CONDITION: Improved

PROGNOSIS: Guarded.

PSYCHIATRIC INCAPACITY: Moderate

MEDICATION: None

During first month of hospitalization, patient exhibited tremendous pressure of speech bizarre behavior and was making grandiose unrealistic plans. She socialized very little with her peers on the ward, keeping mostly to herself. The medication was changed from Mallaril to Thorazine. At the end of thirty days patient had improved somewhat but was still grossly vulgar and uninhibited in her rapport with her peer group on the ward and still has the tendency to confabulate.

The 45-day note indicates that patient was less bizarre and had asked to talk with her counselor. She was no longer verbalizing grandiose plans to go to England and appeared to be in greater control of her behavior. She had a successful home visit and was willing to talk with her counselor. Parents at this point were pressing for discharge. Patient attended the Therapeutic Program provided in the Hospital.

Destination: Parents' home, 81 Fourth Street, Manchester, New Hampshire.

(Continued)

PAGE 3

PRIVILEGED AND CONFIDENTIAL (see page 6)
NEW HAMPSHIRE HOSPITAL

PROGRESS NOTES

PATIENT IDENTIFICATION
RICHARD, Ethel   54322
Adm: 1/21/70   Catholic
                  Tobey Bldg.

Discharge 4-17-71
Re-admission 9-27-76
(after my 2nd return from Burbank)

Ethel C. Richard

Professional <u>Loons on the Loose</u>
The White Coat Government
(OR)
How to REALLY Mess Up Your Kids

There is nothing like a mental institution.
Everywhere you look someone is unhappy or angry or oblivious. Most were normal once and then they gave up.

The first thing I noticed was the old paint peeling off the old sills. I was led into a large area of several rooms within a circle and a door was unlocked and I was put inside a room that had only a mattress and a pail. For three days I was given a tray of food three times a day through a slot in the door of the room.

Once a day I was let out to wash and to empty out my pail. (Lovely job)!

This was definitely a jail from what I could make of it. I told myself that it could be worse. I thought to myself that I could at least have some solitude and being left alone I could think and observe whatever happens there (just in case someday I would write a book just as the one you are now reading).

Strange isn't it how such things sometimes work out?

The bathroom reminded me of an assembly line. Shuffle in a herd of misfits and hurry to get them out in time for the bell. There were lots of stalls and sinks and showers and none of them pretty. It was all very industrial looking and with cold floors. It had an echo but it did not make me want to sing a song.

There were dark brown (painted poop brown) walls and with dingy grime all over them. A slum lord wouldn't want to own it and be put to such a shame. The kids inside seemed normal enough and reminded me of just regular persons who were misunderstood like me.

There was Betty who was very depressed because she knew she would soon turn eighteen and be transferred to another building where they kept the adult women. That building had a lot of very heavily medicated persons who had difficulty staying calm and she wanted to stay with us in Brown building. There were quite a few girls there but I honestly don't remember much about that year. I remember my friend Linda who was a severe epileptic. She was very dopey acting (she always tilted her head in a strange sleepy way and walked stiffly with an odd gait. She was having lots of grand mal seizures and she never talked about anything unless you asked her a question.

Then she gave always a very simple answer without much thought. She had a very simple thought process and was of innocent mentality. She was in a stupor all of the time though. Then there was Annie who was moderately retarded and very emotional. More than once she would get upset and have a tantrum and the aids would come in a group and grab her, giving her a shot and putting her into a strait jacket and locking her inside of her room.

Sandy had palsy and she was overweight and I know she felt depressed. Sheila who was a short and petite girl always

Ethel C. Richard

just behaved like a sweet kid.

There wasn't much to do on the ward. We would play records and maybe do a puzzle or read a magazine. Sometimes some of the girls would play a board game or cards. It was pretty boring at times. We'd all line up to get our meds at the meds station door of the aids office three times a day.

Those of us who smoked cigarettes could carry them with us but we had to get a light from the office staff. (Yes, in those days kids were allowed to smoke cigarettes). Sometimes at early evening we'd watch TV. We'd have to vote on what to watch. In the kitchen the food that was prepared basically tasted like cardboard. We had everything you could want for breakfast but it always tasted like everything else.

Maybe it was the meds taking away my sense of smell or something. Really, whether an egg and sausage or a bowl of oats with milk or lemon pudding, all of the food tasted like dirty dishwater or cardboard.

Between Annie screaming, Linda falling down and Betty crying all of the time it was a bit difficult to concentrate or to sleep at night. The sounds of aids running around and talking together and shutting doors and scuffling after residents who had one emotional problem or another could get slightly disturbing in the night. The aids had a few rules you had to follow like lights out by 8 pm but that did not stop them from running around with flashlights and making sure there was no unusual movement from the residents.

You could hear them talking in the open area outside you door. When I was there during that year I do not remember going to school. There was no going to the movies or

The Bobby Sherman Miracle

swimming. So all of the things Gloria had said to me while at the restaurant were fictitious. I do not remember going outside at all that year. I do not remember any counseling during my first stay which was for fifteen months.

I do have a memory of being wheeled on a cot through hallways and into a room where I saw Linda in a crib just a few feet away from me and having a band around her head that had wires on it. I do not remember being able to move while on that cot. It seems to me that I was strapped into it...

Before I was admitted to the hospital I'd never had a seizure in my life. I had not been feeling dopey or spacey. I had enjoyed long walks all around Manchester and was in excellent physical shape. In the hospital I developed palpitations and weird sensations such as buzzing in my ears and "dropping out" or falling or floating. I started to think weird about things. I became very indifferent to my surroundings and it was like I was actually sleeping while I was awake. I was groggy and did not feel quite right. My voice felt like it did not belong to me. I felt disoriented like I was in a dream state. I felt flat inside.

During my first few weeks inside the hospital I had been very interested in observing persons and trying to figure out whom if anyone I should avoid. I was worried about being inside a mental hospital and not wanting to get too close to some potentially dangerous resident but after a while it seemed like I was not able to differentiate between one person and another.

I became uncaring and that's a very different state of mind than I was in when I was first admitted. Looking at my

Ethel C. Richard

own description here on the page of my state of mind while on drugs while within the hospital, I would have to say that I was without true cognizance or function.

These days I am prone to small seizures when I am very extremely tired. The worse of the problem is that I can be dozing off and get a seizure instead of falling asleep. It's frightening to lie in bed and feel one coming on.

In my case there is a wave or sensation of lightheadedness, tingling throughout the head and heat just before the buzzing within the ears and then you fall into what I can compare to a collapse within yourself.

This is the closest to the sensation of the seizure as I can describe. It's a sinking feeling and you feel a strange jolt between both your inner ears which travels through both sides of your head and down and meeting at the rear of your head at the top of the nape of your neck. It is a zap type of feeling that makes you twitch and can jolt you awake. And in this sense it is very centralized.

It feels like your nerves are overly stimulated and you can actually hear it happening inside your head. That is the wave of the seizure. It lets you know that a seizure is imminent. Once the seizure is subsided you feel exhausted and confused. When I get these symptoms I know that I have been without sleep for too long and have been concentrating or studying too hard. Working at the computer for ten hours will bring one on. I am more than angry at being given a seizure disorder as a result of having been electroshocked while in the hospital.

It was while I was in the hospital that I developed a mean

The Bobby Sherman Miracle

twitch of my nose, eyes (a shutting of eyelids tight and squinting twitch) mouth, tongue and of my hands and arms stiffening up to my shoulders. I twitched a lot and violently.

After I got out of the hospital I remember that I still had the twitch but I do not remember if it was obvious to others while I was on the road later when I ran away to Tucson, Arizona and then on to Bobby in Burbank. When I left Manchester I had no memory whatsoever of my hospital stay and I was not even remotely thinking about or even aware of that twitch.

I know that I had it even after I was discharged from my second hospital commitment in very late 1971 (after I had already met with Bobby several times out at the studios in Burbank). So maybe Bobby remembers a girl with a twitch that came to visit him.

Talk about embarrassment....I would have been mortified to meet him while suffering from a medicinally induced twitching syndrome caused by the Thorazine which I'd been given in the hospital (Tardive Dyskinesia) as I had, if I'd known.

I no longer have an obvious twitch.

I do have some small movement difficulties and severe dexterity problems but I manage to subdue them to a great extent. It takes me a very long time to think and to type these thoughts into this report as I have absolutely horrible finger and hand dexterity.

I am transcribing from memory as accurately as is possible because under scrutiny these things I tell you must be able to be fully grasped by those who would read about them. It takes me hours and hours to write two pages because I am not a fast thinker or a fast typist.

I use two or three fingers at most in order to type and I make typographical errors and must backtrack to fix them. I forget how to spell a word even when I have it solid in my mind.

I have very stiff fingers and believe me that if this work were not so very important I would never put so much energy and hard work into its production as I experience serious stress while I am writing and I do lose my train of thought many times because of petit seizures while I write. I have to constantly bring myself back to the work and re focus on my thoughts.Follow me please and realize the kind of real damage that is caused from electroshock. Would anyone want his or her family member to suffer from these kinds of disability?

Keep this in mind when you are told that your child needs a psychotropic drug or ECT "treatments" by some mental health center or by your child's "psychiatrist" or "behaviorist."

More recently I have been overcome with crying spells that come out of nowhere and I know they are the result of the compounded stress still left from the so called treatments of my long ago stay at the hospital. The kind of crying spells I speak of are just remarkable. They are entirely consuming and yet you don't have a clue why you are crying. It's got to be a stress response.

I am quite functional on a day to day basis. Analyzing the crying (and I've analyzed it frontwards and backwards and in every way I can think of) I believe it's caused from the brain

The Bobby Sherman Miracle

injury I'd received so many years ago.

Just realizing that I have crying spells makes me cry. So, when I get over tired I know to take a break or I'll end up crying uncontrollably or having a seizure while trying to sleep. I am steadfastly working through the process of healing.

I am talking with some very good people such as Dr. John Breeding, PHD Psychologist (he wrote the books, "The wildest Colts Make the Best Horses" and "The Necessity of Madness" and is a founding member of The Coalition for Abolition of Electroshock in Texas) who thoroughly understands the process, having worked with many electric shock survivors. I am encouraged that the tears are coming after all of those years of lost memory and the painful truths of what happened to me that I was not aware of and I had not dealt with because of the sick practices of mainstream psychiatry and how they abuse people as opposed to helping people up and out of their injuries and problems. I have dedicated my history as an asset to help stop involuntary commitment, forced drugging with psychotropic substances and electroshock. Now I will take a break and the next chapter is not decided yet.

Chapter Six

Let's Jump The "S" Monster

Well here it is right in front of me on the page.

The "S" Monster

When I was at the hospital one day I drew a picture which began by my drawing a giant "S" on the paper. I continued to draw and a very scary and odd looking monster appeared when I was finished. I could not figure out what it was that I had drawn. I thought about it over many years but could not put my finger on the meaning of the "S" AND THE HORRIBLE MONSTER I HAD DRAWN on the paper then.

Now I look back at the scary thing I drew mentally and I know exactly what was represented by the drawing. It was the being brought to the electric shock machine and having no power to stop the person from giving me the shocks. I had many shocks that year and that's why I could not remember my stay at the hospital that year after I'd been

Ethel C. Richard

released from the hospital.

There is no greater torture on this planet than electric shock.

For starters, the aid did not tell you where she was bringing you. She would not tell you what they were going to do. The aid would put you in ankle and wrist restraints (which is scary in itself) and you were on a pretty bare cot like a table with a pad. You were wheeled down through a hall and into a room and you could hear the wheels of the table you were lying on as you were moved across the floors. Nobody talked with you. You were alone and feeling spacey and in a zombie type state and just lying there and looking around.

If you were routinely shocked you just closed your eyes oblivious because inside you are helpless. You have no choice and no feelings because the drugs you've been given put you into a kind of deep stupor. You cannot remember what happened yesterday or last week. Still, you are afraid. You clench your fists, your eyes and face and arms in unwilling anticipation of what you know instinctively is coming. The aid puts a thing in your mouth and presses it down and then the gates of hell are opened.

The next thing that happens is that you feel a sharp indescribable buzz type pain throughout your head that has the effect of making you feel on fire and then stiff although you cannot express yourself and then you are unconscious but the whole thing feels like forever because it is so intense. At the same time it happens you see (and feel) an intense flash and then you lose memory of it as well as other memories until the next time it happens to you. It eats you alive.

Physically it twists and breaks your blood vessels and the nerve network within your brain. It creates a violent assault from the inside. It makes me feel severely physically nauseous to remember even to this day. After you've had this so called treatment with electric shock you feel terrified all of the time. It becomes a generalized terror that is with you night and day. Every little thing makes you very jumpy and you have severe terror episodes.

The shock creates an altered mental state of severe confusion and memories immediately evaporate. You lose parts of yourself that you may or may not recover depending on your otherwise physical condition and on how many shocks you actually receive, how close together they are given and the voltages used. Electric shock gives you heart palpitations. I had some very bad palpitations when a teen as a result of them. Another effect of electric shock is that you get severe nightmares and headaches.

Sleep disturbances such as feeling a buzzing heat sensation and complete disassociation from your body, sometimes waking in a conscious but catatonic state. I often had dreams of being followed or attacked by the most horrifying creatures or people. After electroshock people may sleep walk or may talk while sleeping. I used to vocalize loud enough in my sleep to wake others (and myself) up.

The resulting stress from being drugged and electroshocked can be so unbearable that it's easy to understand why some consider that to die is better than to live with the agonizing emotional stress that comes (after the initial numbness) with

Ethel C. Richard

not knowing what is "wrong" with you and why you cannot think straight and the absolute lonesomeness that you are left with. The loneliness is near unbearable because you feel flat and empty and as though absolutely no one can understand your pain (which even you cannot identify the reasons why you cannot function as others are able.

I am an advocate for life and I have been strong in that avenue, but during the days of the hospital and into my early twenties even I fell into occasional thoughts of death and suicide. I in each instance pulled myself up and out of that pit.I have become somewhat of a pull up your bootstraps and get on with life kind of person. I give thanks to God every minute of every day that God has seen fit to give to me.

Electroshock can also make you see and hear things that do not exist simply because the brain has interior burn damage. Depending on what lobes are being burnt on the interior differing senses will be involved in hallucination. Just as in epilepsy there are varying types of seizures, the long term seizures caused from electric shock create like symptoms.

Therefore it is my experienced opinion that electric shock creates a type of manmade epilepsy that must be abolished at all costs for the safety and health of all persons. I am a human being. Why did someone want to create within me the disease of epilepsy?

Chapter Seven

The Criminality of Professional Mainstream Psychiatry

Here I have invited Dr. Breeding to interject his expert knowledge in the field of psychiatry and electroshock to my readers as well as explain the frightening but true answer to this question of criminality in mainstream psychiatry.

My Views on Psychiatry and "Mental Illness"
by John Breeding, PhD

My purpose in this short essay is twofold. The first is to describe my understanding of the nature of psychological distress and emotional healing. The second is to expose the truth about our modern mental health system, call it Psychiatry, which diagnoses citizens as "mentally ill" and "treats" them accordingly.

Ethel C. Richard

On Human Nature

My view is that in order to have even the slightest hope of a clear understanding of psychological distress and healing, one has to have an accurate view of human nature. A paramount truth about humans is that we tend to see the world not as it is, but as we are. To a large extent, our beliefs and assumptions determine how and what we perceive around us. Until they are consciously challenged, the beliefs we hold are determined by what we experienced and learned as developing young people. School, religion, and family have all played major roles in affecting how we now see the world.

Let me briefly illustrate this with a few prime examples. In the United States, we have grown up in a mostly Christian culture. Though Christianity is certainly evolving, most of us are still affected by a tendency to believe that we are born in sin, somehow unworthy and needing to be saved. Add to this the impact of Darwin's ideas about natural selection and the survival-of-the-fittest. This has supported the notion that we need to somehow tame and civilize our naturally aggressive children. Psychology's emphasis on behaviorism, and a school system designed according to these principles, leads us to see humans as born empty, a so-called tabula rasa or "blank slate" waiting to be written upon. Behavior modification (reward and punishment) becomes a primary tool to shape or condition children to be properly socialized. The worst example is that of biological psychiatry, which I will elucidate towards the end of this essay. The bottom line is that we see others and ourselves as inherently sinful, unworthy, aggressive or empty, and we treat each other accordingly. We live in fear and worry, and we lack trust in ourselves.

My own view, and that of many others, is that humans are glorious beings. Our inherent nature is not fundamentally aggressive, unworthy, lazy, irresponsible or dumb. Nor is it empty. The truth is that we are born highly intelligent, zestfully energetic and naturally inclined toward closeness and affection. Just look with fresh eyes at those awesome babies, when their needs are well met, and you will know that.

On Psychological Distress and Emotional Healing

Where does distress come in? Well, take another look at those babies when their needs are not met. The sweet, delightful being disappears and a contorted, crying or screaming creature arrives. We are born with a wonderful true nature, and we are also very very needy and dependent for a long long time. Our development is complex and we need a lot of help.

The process of psychological distress is really quite simple.

1. Our true nature is intelligent, zestful and loving.
2. When we are hurt physically or emotionally, this causes distress (anger, grief, fear, shame, etc.).
3. Distress interferes with true nature. We become less intelligent and less loving.

Ethel C. Richard

That covers most of it. Left unresolved, hurts and distress accumulate, distressing behaviors become chronic, and it becomes easy to see why many people think humans are basically dumb, lazy, irresponsible, and violent.

The good news comes from another aspect of our inherent nature.

1. We have a natural, built-in mechanism, call it emotional discharge, for healing from the effects of hurt.

This healing is accomplished by releasing the effects of the hurt. We discharge hurt and loss by crying, frustration and insult by angry storming, fright by shaking, trembling and sweating, etc. By releasing these distressing emotions, we restore ourselves to our natural intelligence, vitality and loving. We are then able to reconsider and stop living from the unresolved past hurts.

Psychological healing, then, is mostly about finding a safe place and safe people to support the natural process of facing hurts, releasing painful emotion, and letting these things go. This allows an individual to have attention in present time, and to live more and more in the presence of one's own true nature.

Janet Foner, an international leader on issues of mental health system oppression within the Re-evaluation Counseling Community, explains that psychiatry's view on "mental illness" is really a failure to understand the above principles. In her words:

- There is no such thing as "going crazy."
- You can't "lose your mind.:

The Bobby Sherman Miracle

- What is "mental illness" really? It's a very long "session" seeking discharge or having lots of discharge, without a counselor.

One Caveat: Genuine Medical Conditions Can Cause Psychiatric Symptoms

There is one other very important factor to consider, especially with the faces of severe distress, what psychiatry calls "severe mental illness." Though it is a great error to primarily define us as biological or genetic beings, our physicality must be honored and cared for. A host of physical conditions (e.g., blood sugar imbalance, thyroid dysfunction, brain tumor, allergic responses, nutritional deficiency, and so on) can and do cause psychiatric symptoms. It is important to address the physical level of our well-being.

On Biological Psychiatry

Now is the time for part 2 of this essay. I want to provide the basic information necessary to understand the misguided beliefs, and subsequent harmful practices of psychiatry today. As there are millions of homeless people in this country, and as "mental illness" is purported to be a major cause of homelessness, I will focus on how psychiatry treats homeless people. Know, however, that the principles apply to everyone. Our mental health system today is almost entirely guided by a very specific belief system, called biological psychiatry (biopsychiatry). Therefore, The assumptions of biopsychiatry

Ethel C. Richard

have had an enormous impact on modern life. Modeled after the practice of medicine, biopsychiatry has all the trappings of language that we associate with scientific medicine. *Biopsychiatry has the language, but not the science.* To understand psychiatry today, it is necessary to be very clear that it is not about medicine; it is really about social control. The basic assumptions of biopsychiatry are as follows:

1. Adjustment to society is good.
2. Failure to adjust is the result of "mental illness."
3. "Mental illness" (Depression, schizophrenia, bipolar disorder, etc.) is a medical disease.
4. "Mental illness" is the result of biological and/or genetic defects.
5. "Mental illness" is chronic, progressive, and basically incurable.
6. "Mental illness" can (and must) be controlled primarily by drugs; secondarily, and for really severe "mental illness," by electroshock.
7. People with "mental illness" are irrational, and unable to make responsible decisions for themselves; therefore, coercion is necessary and justified.

For a fuller exposition of these seven assumptions, please see my books, *The Wildest Colts Make the Best Horses,* and *The Necessity of Madness and Unproductivity: Psychiatric Oppression or Human Transformation.* For now it is sufficient to recognize that these false beliefs provide the rationale for a coercive "final solution," a logically inevitable expression of a dangerous and distorted worldview. Psychiatry supports and defends the power structure, values, practices and appearances of the status quo; it looks at the world and selects out "defective" individuals for "treatment."

In effect, psychiatry performs a great magic trick. Once an individual is "selected," then everyone is absolved of responsibility. The individual can't help it; he or she is "mentally ill." Everyone else, including society as a whole, is absolved from responsibility. Social justice issues become irrelevant since the problem is said to reside in the defective biology and genetics of the afflicted "mentally ill" individual. The citizen with civil rights becomes the incompetent patient in need of help "for their own good." Anger, dissatisfaction, indignation, and especially refusal to admit their "illness" and accept "treatment (drugs), is called lack of insight and used as evidence that they are indeed "mentally ill." For example, the first question when a homeless "mentally ill" person is experienced as disturbed or disturbing, is: "Have you taken your medication today?"

The Common Ground: Coercion and Control

As I discussed above, shame-based religion, behavioral psychology, and bio psychiatric views of human nature are not remotely compatible with my own. It makes absolutely no sense to glory in children if we arrive in the world empty-minded, or if we are essentially depraved, or if our problems are reducible to defective genetics and biology. But let us

Ethel C. Richard

press on.

The Inquisition was a time when concerned religious folk used extraordinary means to save souls. It is understandable that many see either behavioral psychology or biological psychiatry as a vast improvement over the religion-based attempt to save souls by torture. By comparison, our move into the so-called age of enlightenment, the age of reason, seems a good one. Our faith changed direction, withdrew from religion, and invested in rational, scientific progress. The apparent progress left certain problematic social phenomena very intact.

Thomas Szasz, perhaps the greatest challenger of the false assumptions of biopsychiatry, coined an illuminative analogy about this transition from religion to science.

The Inquisition is to heresy as Psychiatry is to mental illness.

Do you see the connection? Psychiatry replaced religion as society's primary non-judicial means of social control. Both institutions use knowledge not as information, but to define social power; heretics as witches, social challengers, misfits and homeless people as "mentally ill." From such worldviews that see people as inherently shameful or defective, coercion and control are completely justified, absolutely necessary.

Make no mistake about this business of psychiatry. It is a belief system, *not* a science. A large part of our nation has been so successfully conditioned that they believe problems in living are primarily caused by biologically or genetically based

The Bobby Sherman Miracle

"mental illness." We are seeing the results of this way of viewing the world: millions of our precious children on toxic drugs, at the behest of those who they expect to take care of them, and millions more of adults on similar drugs, euphemistically referred to as medication. The reader can *be assured that a country does not deliberately drug millions of its children unless many more millions of adults are on drugs.* It is hard to imagine anything as pathetic.

Mostly unconscious belief systems play a powerful determining role in how we perceive the world and how we respond to what we see. Grossly distorted perceptions of human nature, like that of biopsychiatry, lead to great harm. Since we act according to our beliefs, it is urgent that our beliefs be based in reality. Fortunately, the reality of human nature is really wonderful. Knowing our true nature, trusting in ourselves, ready to resist government psychiatry's false beliefs and coercion, and armed with a little information about the nature of psychological distress and emotional healing, we really can move forward in a good direction. Regarding homelessness, we can then do two things. One is to trust that inherent human nature is most excellent, and responsive to good will, good listening, and good support. Second is to restore our common sense and really tackle issues of jobs and housing.

ELECTROSHOCK
by John Breeding, PhD

"*This is a crime against the spirit. This is a rape against the soul.*"

~ Diann'a Loper
(Electroshock survivor and activist for a ban on ECT)

"*TERROR acts powerfully upon the body, through the medium of the mind, and should be employed in the cure of madness. FEAR accompanied with PAIN and a sense of SHAME, has sometimes cured this disease. Bartholin speaks in high terms of what he calls "flagellation" in certain diseases.*"

~Benjamin Rush
(The "father" of modern psychiatry, whose image today emblazons the official seal of the American Psychiatric Association) (1)

Ethel C. Richard

> *"I open my mouth and the scream surrounds me. My body a lurch and a scream of pain. A firecracker, pain and lights, burning, searing, my bones and my flesh. I am on fire. Shorter than a second. The fragments of a bomb sear my body. Blue-white lights, fiercer than God, going through me É I wondered when they would be over, these ritual burnings. The pain. I would never survive the searing pain. 'Paranoid delusions,' they wrote on my chart. 'She thinks there is a conspiracy to kill her by electrocution.'"*
>
> ~Janet Gotkin *(2)*

(A version of this information has also been published in the Journ 65-79)

Introduction

I deliberately keep this chapter brief because, in my mind, it is a simple issue. Our brains are exquisitely sensitive, and complex -- billions of cells, trillions of connections, more vast and intricate than we can imagine. The most brilliant of our scientists, those who understand more about the brain than any of us, are most humbled and forthcoming about how little they really know about the brain. The most ardent proponents of ECT don't really have a clue as to how it might work. My own point-of-view, like psychiatrist Peter Breggin,

The Bobby Sherman Miracle

neurologist John Friedberg, and others, is that ECT "works" to the extent that it disables the brain.

Psychiatrists call this technique electroconvulsive therapy or ECT. Given that the average ECT procedure induces a level of electricity that is approximately 2 1/2 times greater than that required to induce a convulsion, the term ECT is really a euphemistic misnomer. It is not a "convulsive therapy." Rather, it is systematic brain damage, and the damage is the effect; the more current, the more brain damage. Also known as shock treatment, critics often refer to the procedure as electroshock. Texas, as a result of ardent activism by a coalition of electroshock survivors and concerned allies, is one of the few states to have a systematic reporting system. Official reports on the use of ECT in Texas during fiscal year 1994 included a total of 1,644 patients. (3) The current national estimates are about 100,000 individuals electroshocked each year. After its heyday in the 1940s and 1950s as a means of intimidating and controlling "patients" in state mental hospitals, electroshock lost favor, partly due to the advent of neuroleptic drugs, partly because of the exposure of the horror of it all, as in the popular movie, 'One Flew Over The Cuckoo's Nest'. Most citizens today think that ECT is a relic of bygone days; they tend to be surprised to hear that the practice of ECT is making a resurgence. The American Psychiatric Association is, in fact, working overtime to create an illusion that ECT is no longer even controversial.

Ethel C. Richard

The Need for a Backup Treatment

In most psychiatric settings today, the biological model is a given. With this model, for all intents and purposes, there are only two treatment approaches -- drugs and ECT: drugs for starters and ECT for "treatment-failures" or "treatment-resisters." Thus ECT is the only available back-up treatment when the drugs fail to "work." Psychiatrists would find themselves greatly limited were ECT abandoned or abolished -- they'd have nothing else to offer. Society expects psychiatrists to have the answers, and they readily admit to having them. Nothing would more quickly lower their prestige in the public's eyes, and in their own as well, than to acknowledge not having the answers. The British radical psychiatrist, R.D. Laing, pointed out the irony that while society gives great social police power to psychiatrists, it is equally true that psychiatrists have no choice about whether to exercise that power. In granting the power, society insists that it be used. The coercers are coerced, but so thoroughly conditioned they think they are free.

Doctors are trained to be action-oriented. As a doctor, you just don't stand by and do nothing. There is a reason for the absence of alternatives. Successful outcome of non-medical alternatives would threaten their place in the system; why try something new when the old is paying off so handsomely? Belief that only medical methods are effective is thoroughly ingrained in psychiatrists (that's where their identity is coming from); non-medical alternative approaches are considered inadequate, ineffective and impractical.

The Bobby Sherman Miracle

The Procedure

Electroshock involves the production of a grand mal convulsion, similar to an epileptic seizure, by passing from 70 to 600 volts of electric current through the brain for 0.5 to 4 seconds. Before application, ECT subjects are typically given anesthetic, tranquilizing and muscle-paralyzing drugs to reduce fear, pain, and the risk (from violent muscle spasms) of fractured bones (particularly of the spine, a common occurrence in the earlier history of ECT before the introduction of muscle paralyzers). The ECT convulsion usually lasts from thirty to sixty seconds and may produce life-threatening complications, such as apnea and cardiac arrest. The convulsion is followed by a period of unconsciousness of several minutes' duration. Electroshock is usually administered in hospitals because they are equipped to handle emergency situations which often develop during or after an ECT session.

ELECTROSHOCK MODIFICATIONS

Contrary to claims by ECT defenders, newer technique modifications have made electroshock more harmful than ever. For example, because the drugs accompanying ECT to reduce certain risks raise the seizure threshold, more electrical current is required to induce the convulsion, which in turn increases brain damage. Moreover, whereas formerly ECT specialists tried to induce seizures with minimal current, suprathreshold amounts of electricity are commonly administered today in the belief that they are more effective. (4) Again, the more current, the more brain damage.

ELECTROSHOCK AND ELDERS

The use of ECT is increasing, and seventy percent of the "treatments" are insurance-covered. The bottom line is that more than 100,000 Americans are being electroshocked each year; half are 65 years of age and older, and two-thirds are women. Psychiatry defends the use of electroshock with our elderly women, arguing they need it because of the intractability of geriatric depression. I call it shameful abandonment and mistreatment of our elders, clear evidence of psychiatry as agent of institutionalized ageism and sexism in our society. It is also interesting that here in Texas, our reporting system revealed a 360% increase in the use of ECT between ages 64 and 65.(5) The only logical interpretation is to see it as a dramatic example of how much economics is really the determining factor in the practice; when patients turn 65, doctors can receive Medicare reimbursement for ECT.

PSYCHOLOGICAL EFFECTS

The truth is that electroshock is one of the most dramatic examples ever of iatrogenic (medically-induced) disease. Brain damage, memory loss and mental disability are routine distinguishing results. In addition to obvious physical and mental damage, there are a number of other negative effects of ECT. These include:

The Bobby Sherman Miracle

1) Suppression of emerging distress material;
2) Suppression of ability to heal by emotional release;
3) Creation of emotional distress, including deep feelings of terror and powerlessness;
4) Promotion of human beings in the roles of victims and passive dependents of medical professionals;
5) Confirmation of patient's' belief that there is something really wrong with them (shame).

When I hear of an individual for whom electroshock is being considered, I always ask, "What is important that he or she not remember and tell about?" Or "What is it that the others do not want to hear or look at?" Often it is abuse, always it is difficult, disruptive, threatening, uncomfortable, painful. Emotional discharge is essential to healing. The distress needs to emerge, the truth needs to be told. Electroshock is an awful, violent assault on individuals, and on the possibility of healing by expressing the truth.

Individuals who have undergone ECT report horrific emotional distress resulting from this procedure. Physical and cognitive debilitation, together with intense fear, shame and hopelessness make life and recovery a tremendous challenge for many people who undergo this procedure. My own clients have reported years of fearful avoidance of medical doctors after undergoing electroshock. The fear is so great that they neglect their physical medical needs, rather than go to a doctor. Electroshock survivors often have recurrent nightmares about the electroshock or about symbolic forms of torture and death.

Ethel C. Richard

One client recently shared with me that the reading of testimonials from Holocaust survivors was a key to her recovery; she finally found people whose depth of emotional pain and anguish was similar to her own. This helped her to overcome some of the shame and stigmatization, and to begin walking through the isolation that so many psychiatric survivors experience after their "treatment."

The whole effect of ECT is a waking horror.
Electroshock and Informed Consent

Genuine informed consent for electroshock is nonexistent because electroshock psychiatrists deny or minimize its harmful effects. For example, the American Psychiatric Association officially states, "In light of the available evidence, brain damage need not be included [in the consent form] as a potential risk." (6) In addition, in all but one state ECT may be legally forced upon non consenting individuals who are said to be or are adjudicated mentally unqualified to give their consent.

There are many ways in which informed consent is violated. First, there is denial and minimization of harmful effects. The official APA literature and the typical hospital brochure are both travesties of truth. The consent form example, provided in 1990 by the APA in The Practice of Electroconvulsive Therapy, states that the death rate for ECT is "approximately one per 10,000 patients treated". (7) Publicly available statistics collected between 1993 and 1996 by the Texas Mental Health Department show that the rate is 50 times higher. As noted above, the American Psychiatric

my assertions about medical effects and lack of efficacy, which can be seen in the Appendix.

AUTHENTIC INFORMATION ABOUT ELECTROSHOCK

You are being asked to consider undergoing the psychiatric procedure of electroshock, commonly referred to as electroconvulsive therapy, or ECT. It is your right, according to Texas state law, to be fully informed about the nature and effects of this procedure. Of course, you have a right to refuse the procedure.

Prerequisites to Clear Thinking About Electroshock
STATE OF MIND

A fundamental requisite of good decision making is mental competency. This means that prospective patients are able to understand this information and make a decision. At minimum:

1. Patient is free from the influence of any and all mood-altering substances, including legally prescribed psychotropic medications. 2)Patient is evaluated by a non-psychiatric physician, preferably a neurologist. A mental status examination is required to reveal a well-oriented mind and adequate functioning of higher level decision-making processes.

2. Patient is functionally literate, able to read and comprehend this written material. Alternatively, he or she is able to clearly understand the communication of this material to him or her by audiotape.

STATE OF BODY

A complete physical examination by a non-psychiatric physician, preferably an internist, is recommended. The internist should evaluate for and inform the patient and psychiatrist of the potential for the individual to sustain physical complications of ECT treatment. This is analogous to what internists do in a pre-operative evaluation for surgery.

YOUR CONDITION

You are labeled as "mentally ill," diagnosed with a particular "disease" for which ECT is being recommended as "treatment." ECT is being justified as a "treatment" based on the assertion that your "disease" (probably called Depression, but possibly some other "disease" such as Bipolar Disorder or Schizophrenia) is a biologically or genetically based illness. Your label as "mentally ill" and diagnosis as "Major Depression" or other "mental illness" is entirely hypothetical, based on subjective reports and observations of mood and behavior. There is no evidence of disease, chemical imbalance, or anything physically or chemically abnormal to validate your diagnosis as a medical illness.

The Bobby Sherman Miracle

What It Is
THE PROCEDURE

Electroshock involves the attachment of electrodes to the temples outside one (unilateral) or both (bilateral) frontal lobes, and the administration of electricity to the frontal lobes of the brain. Intensity of voltage may vary from approximately 70 volts to 600 volts. Duration of the electrical current may vary from 0.5 to 4 seconds.

Administration of ECT also varies enormously in number of treatments, from one to literally hundreds over time. A typical course of treatment involves 6 to 12 sessions. Multiple Monitored ECT is one variation which consists of 3 treatments in one session, spaced about 5 minutes apart, with 3 sessions in one week; thus, 9 treatments in one week.

Two pieces of information to know are that:

1) The natural electrical activity of the brain is measured in millivolts, or thousandths of a volt. Thus, the power of ECT is literally hundreds of thousands of times greater than natural brain electrical activity.
2) The average ECT procedure involves a level of electricity that can range from the minimum level required to induce a convulsion up to 40 times greater than that. (11) The official APA recommendation ranges from 1 1/2 to 3 times greater than that required to induce a convulsion. (12)

Ethel C. Richard

DRUGS ADMINISTERED

Electroshock is a procedure which involves administration of the following general classes of medication:

1) general anesthesia
2) tranquilizers
3) muscle relaxants.

Each of these drugs has a wide range of effects on your body, mind and emotions. Listed below is a sample of possible adverse reactions as listed in the Physician's Desk Reference (13):

Anesthesia [i.e. propofol]: circulatory depression, hypotension, hypertension, peripheral vascular collapse, tachycardia, arrhythmia, respiratory depression, cardiorespiratory arrest, skeletal muscle hyperactivity, injury to nerves adjacent to injection site, seizures, hysteria, insomnia, moaning, restlessness, anxiety, nausea, abdominal pain, pain at injection site, salivation and headache.(p. 3416)

Tranquilizer [i.e. valium]: drowsiness, fatigue, ataxia, confusion, constipation, depression, diplopia, dysarthria, headache, hypotension, incontinence, jaundice, changes in libido, nausea, changes in salivation, skin rash, slurred speech, tremor, urinary retention, vertigo, blurred vision, hyperexcited states,anxiety, hallucinations, muscle spasticity, insomnia, rage, sleep disturbance.(p. 2736) Muscle Relaxant [i.e. succinylcholine chloride]: skeletal muscle weakness, profound and prolonged skeletal muscle paralysis resulting in respiratory insufficiency and apnea which require manual or mechanical ventilation until recovery , low blood pressure, flushing, heart attack, bronchospasm, wheezing, injection site reaction, fever.(p. 1091)

You should obtain a list of drugs recommended for ECT, including a complete listing of effects described in the PDR.

FDA CLASSIFICATION

The Federal Food and Drug Administration (FDA) classifies ECT machines as a Type III device. This means that ECT is an experimental procedure, classified in the highest risk category by the FDA. Class III means that the machine has not gone through the rigorous FDA testing required of medical devices, including safety testing and efficacy assessments.

POSSIBLE MEDICAL EFFECTS OF ECT

1. Death
2. Brain Damage
3. Cardiovascular Complications
4. Extra Risk for the Elderly
5. Seizures and Epilepsy
6. Memory Loss

Note: Because ECT is a high-risk experimental procedure and because of the possibility of permanent brain damage, you may want to consider magnetic resonance imagery (MRI) brain scans before and after this procedure. Pre- and post-MRI's are one way to measure the possible physical effects of ECT on your brain.

EMOTIONAL EFFECTS

1) Terror
2) Shame
3) Helplessness
4) Hopelessness

Many individuals who have undergone ECT report horrific emotional distress resulting from this procedure. Physical and mental debilitation, together with intense fear, shame and hopelessness often make life and recovery a tremendous challenge for people who undergo this procedure.

LACK OF EFFICACY

Research indicates the following:
1) No lasting beneficial effects of ECT. (14)
2) Sham-ECT (where an individual is anesthetized and told they will receive ECT, but actually do not) has the same short term outcomes as actual ECT. (15))/ Research clearly shows that ECT does not prevent suicide. Suicide rates for those receiving ECT are no lower than non-ECT patients with similar diagnostic profiles.

The Bobby Sherman Miracle

FINANCIAL DISCLOSURE

The cost of ECT varies significantly. Cost of the procedure itself may vary from $100 to $300 per treatment for the psychiatrist's bill. "Hidden" costs include fees for the anesthesiologist and the surgery suite (up to $800 combined per session), room and board at the hospital (usually $800 to $1300 per day at a private psychiatric hospital), psychotherapy charges by the psychiatrist (average $100 - $150 per hour), consultant fees, and charges for whatever drugs you will be administered. Depending on the setting and whether you are inpatient or out-patient, there will be variable fees for the "operating room" and the hospital. You should obtain a full financial disclosure of all costs in writing, prior to decisions about any procedure.

Endnotes

Quoted in Frank, L.R., ed., I nfluencing Minds: A Reader in Quotations. Feral House, 1995.

Gotkin, J. T oo Much Anger, Too Many Tears. Quadrangle Press: NY, 1975.

Publicly available statistics from the Texas Department of Mental Health and Mental Retardation, 1994.

Cameron, D. ECT: Sham Statistics, the Myth of Convulsive Therapy, and the Case for Consumer Misinformation. Journal of Mind and Behavior, 1994, 15, 177-198.

Texas Department of Mental Health and Mental Retardation Report, 1996.

Ethel C. Richard

American Psychiatric Association task force report, The Practice of Electroconvulsive Therapy, 1990.

Ibid.

Wisconsin Coalition for Advocacy (WCA) ÔInformed Consent for Electroconvulsive Therapy: A Report on Violations of Patients' Rights by St. Mary's Hospital, Madison, Wisc.Ó 1/17/95. WCA, 16 N. Carroll St., Madison, Wisc. 53703.

Benedict, A. & Saks, M. *The Regulation of Professional Behavior: Electroconvulsive Therapy in Massachusetts. The Journal of Psychiatry and Law, 1987,15,2,247-275.*

Baughman, F. *E-mail correspondence, September 10, 1998.*

Sackeim, H., et al *Stimulus Intensity, Seizure Threshold and Seizure Duration. P sychiatric Clinics of North America, 1991,14,4,803-843.*

American Psychiatric Association, 1990. (See above)

Physician's Desk Reference: 53rd Edition. Montvale, NJ: Medical Economics Co., 1999.

Rifkin, A. *ECT versus tricyclic antidepressants in depression: A review of evidence . Journal of Clinical Psychiatry, 1988,49,1, 3-7. Consensus Conference on ECT, 1985.* Reported by Peter Breggin in B rain-Disabling Treatments in Psychiatry, 1997, p. 135.

Crow, T. and Johnstone, E. *Controlled trials of electroconvulsive therapy. Annals of NY Academy of Sciences, 1986,462,12-29.*

The Bobby Sherman Miracle

Additional Resources

Breggin, P. (1991) Shock Treatment is not Good for Your Brain, in Toxic Psychiatry. New York: St. Martin's Press.

Breggin, P. (1997) Electroshock and Depression, in Brain Disabling Treatments in Psychiatry. New York: Springer Publishing.

Frank, L., ed. (1978) The History of Shock Treatment. Available from Leonard Frank, 2300 Webster St., San Francisco, CA, 94115. ($12 postpaid)

Frank, L. (1990) Electroshock: Death, Brain Damage, Memory Loss, and Brainwashing. Journal of Mind and Behavior, 11, nos. 3 & 4.

Friedberg, J. (1976) Shock Treatment Is Not Good For Your Brain. San Francisco: Glide. Friedberg, J. (1977) Shock Treatment, Brain Damage and Memory Loss: A Neurological Perspective. American Journal of Psychiatry, 134, 9, 1010-1013.

ShockWaves, Linda Andre editor, Committee for Truth in Psychiatry, PO Box 1214, New York, NY 10003. (212) 473-4786 This is an important newsletter for information related to ECT.

Dendron, David Oaks publisher, PO Box 11284, Eugene OR, 97440. (503) 341-0100. The best newspaper available on mental health system oppression. David Oaks is also the contact point for Support Coalition International, an umbrella group of organizations devoted to the work of mental health liberation. Their website is www.efn.org/~dendron. Psychiatry, Victimizing the Elderly, a booklet by the Citizens Commission on Human Rights (CCHR), 6362 Hollywood Blvd., Suite B, Los Angeles, CA 90028. In Texas, call 1-800-572-2905. For other states call

Ethel C. Richard

1-800-869-2247. CCHR is a private, non-profit organization whose sole purpose is to investigate and expose psychiatric violations of human rights.

www.banshock.org, a website on the internet devoted to making information available regarding electroshock treatment and attempts to ban or restrict its use. Many links to other useful sites.

Appendix

*Electroshock Annotated Bibliography
by Moira Dolan, MD*

EFFECTS OF ELECTROCONVULSIVE THERAPY:
A review of the scientific literature

DEATH

In a large retrospective study of 3,288 patients getting ECT in Monroe County, NY, ECT recipients were found to have an increased death rate from all causes. Babigian, H., et al. Epidemiologic Considerations in ECT. *Arch Gen Psych* 1 984;4:246-253.

Survival in 65 patients hospitalized and treated for depression was evaluated by researchers at Brown University. They reported that the 37 patients who received ECT had survival rates of 73.0% at one year, 54.1% at two years, and 51.4% at three years. In contrast, depressed patients who did not receive ECT had survival rates of 96.4%, 90.5% and 75.0% at 1,2 and 3 years respectively. Kroessler, D. and Fogel, B.

The Bobby Sherman Miracle

Electroconvulsive Therapy for Major Depression in the Oldest Old. A m J Geriatr Psych 1 993;1:1:30-37.

The risk of death was doubled in depressed patients who got ECT in a seven year follow up study of 188 patients.

O'Leary, D. and Lee, A. Seven Year Prognosis in Depression - Mortality and Readmission Rates in the Nottingham ECT Cohort. British J of Psychiatry 1996; 169: 423 - 429.

The first three years of mandated recording of death within 14 days of ECT in the state of Texas yielded reports of 21 deaths. Eleven of these were cardiovascular, including massive heart attacks and strokes, three were respiratory, and six were suicides. *Don Gilbert, Commissioner, Texas Department of Mental Health and Mental Retardation, 1996.*

BRAIN DAMAGE

Over twenty years ago Cotman reported in *Science* t hat ECT disrupts (protective) protein production by brain cells. More recent studies show that electric shocks to the brain also causes an increase the production of inflammatory proteins inside brain cells. *Cotman, et al. Electroshock effects on brain protein synthesis. S cience 1 971;178:454-456. Marcheselli, et al. Sustained induction of prostaglandin endoperoxide synthase - 2b yseizuresin hippocampus JBiol Chem 1996; 271:24794-24799.*

C. Edward Coffey, MD, a leading proponent of ECT, conducted a study at Duke University Medical Center and the Durham VA Hospital which looked at the brain scans (by MRI) of patients before and after ECT. Out of 35 patients studied, 8 had changes on MRI after shock. That's 22%, or greater than one in 5, with anatomic brain effects. Among those with the brain changes, one patient suffered a stroke and two had new abnormal neurologic signs on exam within 6 months of the ECT.

Coffey, et al. Brain Anatomic Effects of ECT *Arch Gen Psych* 1991;48:1013-1021.

Weinberger looked at the effects of ECT on the brains of schizophrenics by comparing brain CT scans of those who had ECT with schizophrenics who never received shock. He documented that cerebral atrophy (brain shrinkage) was significantly more common in those who had been shocked.

Weinberger, et al. Structural abnormalities in the cerebral cortex of chronic schizophrenic patients. Arch Gen Psych 1979; 36: 935 - 939 .

Another CT scan study done by Calloway looking at a similar group confirmed that frontal lobe atrophy (brain shrinkage) was significantly more common in ECT recipients.
Calloway, et al. ECT and cerebral atrophy: a CT study. Acta Psych Scand 1 981;64:442-445.

Andreasen used MRI scans to demonstrate a strong correlation between the number of previous ECT treatments to enlarged ventricles (loss of brain tissue).
Andreasen, et al. MRI of the Brain in Schizophrenia Arch Gen Psych 1 990;47:35-41.

A study in England compared the brain CT scans of 101 depressed patients who had received ECT to 52 normal volunteers. They found a significant relationship between treatment with ECT and brain atrophy. In fact ECT recipients were twice as likely to have a measurable loss of brain tissue in the front area of the brain and a tripling of the incidence of a loss *of brain tissue in the back of the brain. M ost significantly, the brain abnormalities correlated only with ECT, and not with age, alcohol use, gender, family history of mental illness, age at the time of psychiatric diagnosis, or severity of mental illness. (quoted words are those of the study authors)*

Dolan, RJ, et al. The cerebral appearance in depressed subjects P sychol Med 1986;16:775-779.

An animal study sought to discover whether giving supplementary oxygen during shock would prevent brain damage; they also gave vitamin E to lessen the effects of damaging 'free radical' molecules that get released during a shock seizure. They found no difference in the brain damaging effects of ECT-induced seizures by giving oxygen and vitamin E. These findings disprove the claim that modern ECT methods (complete with anesthesia and oxygen) are any less damaging to the brain than uncontrolled seizures.

Manoel, et al. Brain damage following repeated electroshock in cats and rats Rev Rom *Neurol Psych 1986; 24: 59 - 64 .*

CARDIOVASCULAR COMPLICATIONS

ECT-induced seizures cause a rapid rise in blood pressure; at the same time the brain experiences a significant reduction in blood flow.

Webb, et al. Cardiovascular response to unilateral ECT Biol Psych *1 990;28:758-766 . Rosenberg, et al. Effects of ECT on cerebral blood flow C onvulsive Therapy 1 988;4:62-73.*

A Mayo clinic study of 34 elderly patients receiving shock found an 18% incidence of serious heart arrhythmias during treatment; 4 had ventricular tachycardia requiring IV lidocaine,

Ethel C. Richard

2 had supraventricular tachycardia requiring IV beta blockers. An additional 2 patients had other cardiogram changes.
Tomac, T. and Rummans, T. Safety and Efficacy of Electroconvulsive Therapy in Patients Over Age 85. A m J Geriatr Psych 1 997;5:126-130.

After his eighth ECT, a 57-year-old man died of heart rupture.
Ali, P.B. and Tidmarsh, M.D. Cardiac Rupture During Electroconvulsive Therapy Anesthesia 1997; 52: 884 - 895.

Physicians from Tulane University Medical School reported on a 69-year-old woman who developed brain hemorrhage during ECT. She was also left with epilepsy afterward. This was, as expected, associated with further deterioration in her mental status from her baseline depression. They conclude that the fragile vessels of the elderly may make some patients a particularly high risk for ECT.
Weisberg, et al. Intracerebral hemorrhage following ECT. Neurology 1 991; Nov: 1849.

EXTRA RISKS IN THE ELDERLY

In an analysis of 34 persons over the age of 85 who were subjected to ECT, researchers at the Mayo clinic documented that 79% suffered treatment complications, including a 32% incidence of confusion and delirium, 67% incidence of transient high blood pressure, 18% incidence of serious heart arrhythmias during treatment, 2 patients with other cardiogram changes, 3 with falls, 1 hip fracture due to fall.

Tomac, T. and Rummans, T. Safety and Efficacy of Electroconvulsive Therapy in Patients Over Age 85. A m J Geriatr Psych 1997; 5:126-130. ECT-enthusiast Dr. Coffey and his associate Dr. Figiel found that 10 out of 87 (that's 11% of) elderly patients getting ECT for depression remained *delirious between ECT sessions for no discernible medical reason other than the ECT itself.* (Italicized words are those of the study authors.) They documented by brain MRI scans that 90% of these unfortunate patients had lesions in the basal ganglia areas of the brain, and 90% also had moderate to severe white matter lesions.

Figiel, Coffey, et al. Brain MRI findings in ECT-induced delirium J of Neuropsych and Clin Sci 1990;2:53-58.

Kroessler and Fogel's 1993 study on death rates reported above was done on the "oldest old," depressed patients at least 85 years of age. Mortality rates were significantly greater for those who received ECT, compared to those who did not. *Kroessler, D. and and Fogel, B. Electroconvulsive Therapy for Major Depression in the Oldest Old.* Am J Geriatr Psych 1 993;1:1:30-37.

EPILEPSY

In a review of the literature on the well-known ECT complication of epilepsy, researchers calculated *that the* a ge-adjusted incidence of new seizures after ECT was fivefold greater than the incidence found in the non-psychiatric population. (italicized words are those of the study authors)

Devinsky, O. and Duchowny, M.S. Seizures after convulsive therapy: A retrospective case survey. Neurology 1 983;33:921-5.

Persistent brain wave disruption to the point of status epilepticus has been reported to occur following ECT. Individual reports by Drs. Weiner and Varma on different patients both describe acute disorientation and deterioration of intellectual function immediately following ECT. This was found to be due to ongoing epileptic brain wave forms that was initiated by the ECT.

Weiner, R.D. Prolonged confusional states and EEG seizure activity following ECT and lithium use. Am Journal Psych 1980 ; 137 : 1452 - 1453 . Varma, N.K. et al. Nonconvulsive status epilepticus following ECT. Neurology 1 992;42:2263-264.

MEMORY LOSS

Publicly available data from the state of California's Department of Mental Health reveals that over 99% of ECT recipients complain of memory loss 3 months following treatment, with the average number of ECT sessions being 5 to 6.

A. Lazarow, Chief, Office of Human Rights, California Department of Mental Health, 1996.

In a chapter on the cognitive effects of ECT in a psychiatry textbook, Sackheim indicates that cognitive effects (disordered thinking), particularly amnesia, can be long lasting after shock. Sackeim, in Cognitive Disorders: Pathophysiology and Treatment, edited by Moos, et al 1992.

The conclusion that amnesia can be a long lasting effect of shock is arrived at by both Squire and Weiner in separate studies. Squire, et al. Retrograde amnesia and bilateral ECT: Long term follow-up. Arch Gen Psych 1981; 38: 89 - 95 .

Weiner, et al. *Effects of stimulus parameters on cognitive side effects* Ann NY Acad Sci 1986;462:315-325.

LACK OF EFFICACY

In the large NY study cited earlier, the death rates from suicide among depressed patients given ECT were slightly higher at the 1 year mark. By 5 years the suicide rate was the same for depressed patients who got ECT as those who didn't.

Babigian, H., et al. *Epidemiologic considerations in ECT.* Arch Gen Psych 1984;41:246-253.

In a University of Iowa study of treatment effectiveness, 1,076 depressed patients were categorized according to whether they received ECT, or high doses of antidepressant medications, or low doses of antidepressant medications, or neither (ECT nor meds). Long term follow up revealed that all groups had the same suicide rates, indicating that the incidence of suicide is not affected by treatment. The authors conclude: "Therefore, active biological treatments, such as ECT, may not be deemed as 'lifesaving' now as in the past."

Black, et al. *Does treatment influence mortality in depressives?* Ann Clin Psych 1989;1:165-173.

The same findings are documented in three other studies: ECT does not prevent suicide in depressed patients.

Eastwood, et al. *Seasonal patterns of suicide, depression, and ECT.* Br J Psych 1976;129:472-475.

Babigian, et al. *Epidemiological considerations in ECT.* Arch Gen Psych 1984;41:216-253.

Milstien, et al. *Does ECT prevent suicide?* Convulsive Therapy 1986;2:3-6.

PART TWO

Chapter Eight

Living in a Fear Filled Fog
Born to be Wild

I left the hospital in a fog. If I'd been sent home with a prescription it certainly would not have mattered because we did not have any money to buy meds. My parents were still together and so we could not get welfare to purchase psych drugs. The bottom line is that I was free to not take them even if I had them.

After my stay in the hospital my folks really did not give a damn if I took the drugs or not. I did not remember the hospital and I was seriously walking in a crazy haze of indifference and isolation from people. I felt as if I had no ties to the people I lived with except that I liked my brother Eddie.

I felt misunderstood and very much like I was different from everyone I knew. Truthfully, I had a good point there. I was definitely very different from those in my family in

Ethel C. Richard

basically every way after having lived through the life which I have already laid bare for you. I was extremely lonely and not taking any drugs whatsoever (other than my nicotine) and I was not interested in the life that was laid out for me.

I could only see one outcome…that I would be stuck in a go nowhere life. At my house there was no discussion about anything of importance to family life. My family just continued as though nothing had happened and nothing was going to change. There was a family member who came to see me one day.

I do not exactly remember who she was (maybe an aunt on my Dad's side of the family) and she asked me a few questions. I told her that I was "different" (in my heart I was thinking "more serious and mature" than other people, but she answered back with "what do you mean by different? You are a "pretty" girl….!"

I shook my head in disgust at her limited attitude. How could people be so shallow as to think that I was worried about my looks? Nothing was about being pretty. It was all about being real, a genuine and serious person who wanted to live and not be totally stifled and stuffed inside a coffin without ever having had a chance to live. Her visit with me only made me feel lonelier.

I was dealing with people outside my doors who always wanted to hang with me and who were talking about the things they were doing and what had happened to them. One of the girls showed up in a cast and a sling and she told me that her boyfriend had been fooling around and had set her on fire when he was playing with lighter fluid and a lighter.

The Bobby Sherman Miracle

I'd met Bruce and had seen his odd behavior before and so I also had reason to be wary because he appeared to be unbalanced and dangerous.

I'd gone with some of the kids to the landfill area of town in a car and there was a 12 foot high fence with a narrow opening (too narrow to drive through) which blocked off a very large open area and one of the boys decided that, "gee wouldn't it be cool to get this car through the narrow opening of the fence?" (he'd been drinking) and we ended up all still in the car with its passenger side doors stuck up in the air between the fence posts. I and another girl managed to climb out through a window and stood around and talking together about "how stupid the boys are" and "how would we get back to Manchester"? The scenario that I just explained involved only drinking and being stupid but it was not my cup of tea and I hated boys and men from Manchester because from what I could see they were complete morons. We had to walk back and I was not too happy.

So, I got it in my head that I would find someone older and maybe a bit more mature to get to know.

I met this guy who was about 25 years old who rode around on a fancy motorcycle and he wanted to take me for a ride. We went to his home and he lived with his mom and so I was not so worried. We went to his room and we talked for awhile and then he pulled out some things I had not been expecting to see. He pulled out baggies of white powder, melted the powder and he wrapped his arm tightly with the belt, took a syringe, and

Ethel C. Richard

gave himself a shot. I got a real lesson in "do not trust people that you've never met before". (It did not matter that I should have learned a lesson from my bad experiences in Manchester before this, because I could not remember what had happened to me in Manchester before. The shock machines had wiped out all of my memory of that experience.

Over the course of a week or so I ran into other members of the motorcycle gang. This same man was coming around and insisted that I come to see him. He was talking with me while sitting in the park on his Harley when others on bikes also drove up and started talking with him. So, here was a group of men and one of them with a female rider who was dressed in the same kind of leather gear and looking pretty tough. I had seen her somewhere I said to myself (she looked familiar) and I looked her over closely. She was also talking and she did not seem threatening toward me and for some reason the men were not bothering me but acted like I belonged with the man who had asked me out again.

I was stupid and I went along because of the pressure to go. I climbed on his bike and we went to a location downtown where there was a rooming house and a party going on inside.

There were something like 20 people crowded into a room. They were all smoking dope and drinking and talking. Some were looking at and talking about stuff they had in bags. One guy held up a baggie and was talking about passing it around. I just kept to myself and talked very little. I stuck close to the man who brought me in so that nobody else would try to talk with me. Suddenly the woman who had come in with us verbally opened her mouth against me and was about to fly physically into me to grab me and throw me around. She said some crazy thing about me eying her boyfriend and was about to lunge into me when her boyfriend swung around to stop her. He grabbed her arm and told her to leave me alone.

Luckily for me she backed off. She was huge and I would have been seriously disfigured if she'd pulled her knife (She had a knife visible on her belt). She looked at me like she wanted to hurt me. I did not want a run in with that one....

That was the last I saw of him or that gang. I got home and was determined to not be hanging around Manchester anymore. The roughneck elements were very much leaving a bad taste in my mouth. I told Jack (who'd hooked up with me again after I was discharged from the hospital) that I couldn't handle Manchester and had to get out fast.

Ethel C. Richard

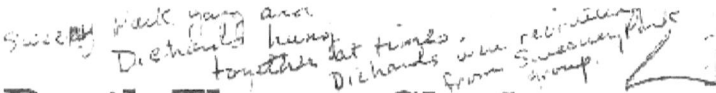
[handwritten annotation:] Sweeney Park gang and Diehards hung together at times — we recently [illegible] Diehards from [illegible] group

Death Threats Shadowed New Hampshire Prosecutor

By CISSY TAYLOR
Union Leader Staff

Manchester attorney James Connor understands full well the dangers faced by those in the judicial system who take it upon themselves to "keep peace in our community and keep crime out of it."

In the 1970s, Connor spent nearly a year with state troopers and Manchester police guarding him day and night because officials believed an outlaw motorcycle gang wanted to assassinate him.

By the end of Connor's tour as Hillsborough County Attorney, 42 members of the Manchester-based Diehards had been sent to prison on a variety of charges including rape and murder.

One of the murder victims, 18-year-old Wanda Graham, had been shot three times in the head before her body was dumped in Bedford.

Another rape victim was killed before the case went to trial, apparently in hopes the rapists could avoid prison. But, Connor said, because she had testified at the probable cause hearing, the case was carried through without the victim. The Diehard rapists were convicted.

It began, as Connor remembered yesterday, in the early '70s when a Manchester woman was gang-raped by several members of the Diehards, a Queen City-based motorcycle gang.

The gang rape was particularly brutal, Connor said. The victim's arm was broken and at one point, a pistol was put in her vagina.

Manchester police came to Connor, who had been county attorney since 1968, and explained what had transpired.

"There seemed to be a burgeoning show of force ... by the Diheards," Connor said. "There were a number of cases in which they were involved."

Five members of the Diehards were convicted of rape and committing unnatural acts.

It was the beginning of the end for the Diehards. And, it was the end of a life of privacy for Connor for a time.

"I was at my home outside of Manchester when two state troopers came to my door," he said.

Federal officials and then-Attorney General Warren Rudman had determined that the Diehards were making plans to kill Connor.

"I was not too pleased to hear that," he said, "nor to hear that they would be with me around the clock. It was so foreign to me."

Connor, who ironically had not wanted to seek one more term as county attorney, relented when convinced by Rudman that the threats were serious.

The gang, Connor was told, had a chillingly large amount of information about Connor, his life and his activities.

"It was not my choice," he said, "but I really respected what Warren said."

Connor added: "I think I was more puzzled than frightened by it. It was more an affront to the system than it was to me as an individual."

He did, however, acknowledge that he was uncomfortable sometimes driving home to a rural house, "cars following me, turning the same way I was."

"I had to carry a gun for a while, which I was very bothered by," he said.

Maybe even more disturbing were the Christmas cards, sent by members of the Diehards, noting they were "thinking of me."

What concerns Connor more today, however, is the death of Paul R. McLaughlin, the 42-year-old assistant attorney general in Massachusetts.

In Connor's years as a prosecuting and private practice attorney, there is one thing he has learned is a certainty.

"Everything that happens in Massachusetts eventually happens here."

NH Reacts With Sympathy, Determination

By CISSY TAYLOR
Union Leader Staff

Prosecutors and other law enforcement officials said, a change that came about as Howard and his staff began to see the changing face of crime in the

---

I did not remember Jack from before the hospital when he'd first been discharged from the army but he had been hanging around some and talking about his recent conversion to Christianity and getting me involved in Bible Studies and prayer meetings. I was listening to him when he talked about

The Bobby Sherman Miracle

the House of Maranatha in Tucson and about how God could change my life and give to me a better future. His was your basic, "accept Jesus into your heart and be born again" type message. I decided to trust him and I told him that I had too much trouble in Manchester and wanted out. He gave to me a highway map he'd routed to Tucson, Arizona and told me that there were good people at the study commune and that he'd let them know I was coming to stay with them.

I told only one other person that I was leaving Manchester. She was a street gang member who liked my father. She got pissed off because I told her I was blowing the state and would not be returning. As I've stated earlier in this book, the day before I left town I was cornered in the park by the whole gang while I was walking to the store. They gathered into a circle and closed off the area. The particular gang member stood in front of me and told me, "You are not running away from home... You are not going to do that to your father."

The behind the scene story here is that this gang girl I was told by my uncle was having an affair with my Dad. My uncle had approached me for sex and told me that he would not hurt me and that he'd give me money. I was repulsed by him and very angry and told him to NEVER talk to me that way ever again or that I will tell his wife. He replied with, "Why not? You're father does it with your girlfriends…"

I had not thought of my father that he was messing around with anyone and certainly not that thirteen year old monster that was then standing in front of me and telling me to not hurt my Dad.

When I'd tried to tell Dad what his brother had done he

Ethel C. Richard

laid into me and yelling at me said, "Shut up!

Don't talk about my brother like that!

Thereafter I started noticing that my Dad and that person had been talking together and acting chummy, which before Dad's brother had said those things to me I had not noticed. There was no way that I was staying in Manchester and I told her that I'd had enough of the crap going on around there and I wanted a real life. She took a swing at me and me being very small and she being made of muscle, huge and husky.

I went down on the pavement hitting my head. She straddled me and pinned me by my shoulders to the pavement with her knees. I could not get a swing in and I was pulverized. Not a prayer of defending myself. She just kept punching me in the head until I was knocked unconscious. I saw everybody from the gang looking like it was a show and jeering and then I realized that I was bleeding and that I was probably done for. But then after, it did not even bother me. I woke up and no one was there and I went home and there I must have cleaned up (I do not remember). I do know for sure that I saw Jack and got the map and hit the road at precisely Four pm on Friday, May 14, 1971.

I had no intention of ever looking back.

Chapter Nine

Searching For a Better Life
in a Wicked World

Mom used to tell me that there were more wicked people in the world than good. Every once in awhile she would say something insightful to me like, she'd say, "There is no difference between black and white. There are good people and there are bad people. But there are more wicked people in the world than good."

At other times she would say something to me that would come from right out of nowhere and be shocking to me, causing me to question things in general but not at all openly. Like when I was about 10 years old when Mom totally floored me with the instruction, "Never take your pants down to a boy." (Talk about embarrassing ....I flinch to even expose this moment that occurred between my Mom and I within this story). When I asked her "Why Mommy?"

She simply replied, "Just don't do it."

Well that was the extent of my sex education at home. I

Ethel C. Richard

never received another word ever from Mom and I never asked another question about it again. Once when I was twelve years old and I had just begun to have my monthly visitor I was watching TV one afternoon with Dad and he suddenly turned to me and said, "Grow up to be a good woman."

I believe that my parents both tried to raise me right but that their parenting skills were very limited. They were the product of their generation. Nobody was open about sex and relationships in those days. (At least not in Manchester) I had a cousin who thought that she was pregnant because she had only kissed a boy. Catholic girls had trouble in those days to get solid information as we grew up about such subjects of sex as the subjects themselves were taboo to bring up even to our parents. I was a quiet and thoughtful kid. I would pick pussy willows and Lilacs for Mom and bring them home to Mom because I knew she liked them and I did not want to see her crying (sometimes she would cry, like when my grandpa died or when we sometimes did not have any heat in our home and we had to wear our coats to bed). I would help Mom make the fudge that Dad liked because I wanted to see my Dad's look of surprise and happiness when he got fudge from us.

Dad would sing the Flintstones theme in the mornings while shaving in the bathroom and he would do a little jig while singing that made me feel happy to watch him playing like that. (I would come in and watch him shave just to listen to him sing the song and wiggle around). I loved my Dad like crazy and that's probably why I "inherited" (emulated) some of his habits, even the bad ones. I became very independent

The Bobby Sherman Miracle

mostly because I was oldest of the kids at home and I was not stopped from doing my thing which I loved both male and female type pastimes.

I gravitated to my Dad and many times I felt bad for him because Mom was very strict and would not approve of things that Dad liked to do which made him feel lonesome. I knew he was depressed having to work in the factory and unable to really give to us what would have made us happy as kids. He wanted to bring us to places like Disneyland and Expo but there just was not enough money for those things. He would get depressed and have a few beers and Mom would become discontent and nagging about his behavior and he would get fed up and make a dive for the door.

I remember once when I was nine years old that he took for the door and I was so worried that he'd get into an accident and never come home that I blocked the door with my body and begged him to please not go while I was crying my eyes out. He left anyway and I held it against my Mom that Dad had trouble to be happy at home with us because my Mom was too straight laced and strict to accept that maybe it was ok for Dad to have a drink when he got home from work. Mom had the same attitude toward swearing, cigarettes and poker. Mom hated them too and she made her opinions very well known to us.

Her attitude also reflected in the bedroom. (The reason why I was fearful sometimes when I was very young and heard Dad angry with Mom when they were in their bedroom and I would cry out to Dad to please "Don't hurt Mommy!")…Mom was also too strict in marital relations and

Ethel C. Richard

would rather fight than show sexual affection and acceptance of my father's preferences which were in line with what is normally expected within marriage.

I decided that to be Baptist was not my thing. I loved my Mom but I was totally against her ideals especially because they were hurting my Dad and creating problems in our home. As I've already iterated in a previous chapter Mom began telling me things as I got older like, "You are Dad's favorite but you've always been the black sheep of the family." When she said these things to me I resented it.

It should not be surprising that these things put together created within me the deep desire for a sweet, affectionate and caring family environment to exist at home. Since it did not exist in my home I began thinking about what it might be like to have a happy home free of all the stress I'd experienced in mine. I fantasized about it to the point that by the time I turned nine I would shut my door and not come out for long periods of time and just envision what my idea of a happy life would be like.

We moved around so much that every time we got to a new apartment we would turn it into a picnic event. We'd buy sandwich fixings and sit around having lunch in our "new "kitchen drinking soda and having a ball. I particularly liked liverwurst and looked forward to moving because I knew we would get some. Dad was French and he liked blood sausage. So didn't I and I enjoyed watching him fry it up. It was a big deal when we got cheese or ice cream.

Some of the happiest times that I remember revolved around our moving which we did on average once every six

The Bobby Sherman Miracle

months to a year when I was a child. I had to get good at letting go of friends I'd made every time we moved. To have emotional attachments with persons I'd gotten to know would have hurt too much and I made it my policy from a young age to not take the friendships I'd made too seriously.

I at some point while still very young picked up a habit of making repetitious behaviors. I had a weird obsession of numbers in walking and movements. You know that old childhood phrase some of us used to say in play when walking on a sidewalk…? (Don't step on a crack it cause it will break your mother's back) Well I developed a nervous habit of never allowing myself to step on a crack when on a sidewalk. I also counted by habit (up to the number eight) and then repeatedly did it when I washed my hands or went to the bathroom. Talk about odd behavior…! Don't they call this kind of behavior obsessive compulsive?

But what do they know? I think that I was simply trying to comfort myself in an odd form of self-assurance of security that (at least something) could be counted on, even if it was just me doing the counting…! I was very insecure at that time in my young life.

Reading About Bobby Sherman in a Magazine

Sometime in my thirteenth year I had picked up my first ever copy of a teen celebrity magazine from the store. I checked out all of the stories about the then popular teen idols and none of them really stood out at me or got my interest except for a story I'd read about Bobby that talked about how he'd been insecure as a kid because of moving allot and that he'd been dropped as a baby and had gotten a broken collarbone and had

Ethel C. Richard

also stuttered when younger. I read more about Bobby and the article said that he liked psychology in school and had a photo development table at home.

It also said that he'd made a large scale replica of a Disneyland display in his yard and charged 10 cents admission and gave the money to charity when he was a boy. The article also talked about how he could play many musical instruments and mentioned that he had great morals as well as talents and that he was looking for a good girl to form an eventual family with. After I'd read all of these very nice materials about him I decided that I would like to know more about him and so I began buying the magazines so that I could get as much information on him as possible.

I read about his family and about his life growing up and realizing that he must have started from a very poor background like me, I made the decision that I must somehow meet him because he and I it appeared had a very lot in common and perhaps could understand each other and that maybe he was the man I was supposed to marry but that I would never know and never have a chance to even find out if I did not somehow get to where he was. I felt very strongly about this and in my heart and in my prayers I thought about Bobby and asked God to help me at least meet him and see where it goes.

In my mind there was no question that Bobby was a very straight and caring, intelligent unusual man. He seemed to me like someone truly worthy of my pursuit of getting to know him better and not just on the level of reading about him. I wanted a serious man. Bobby Sherman

The Bobby Sherman Miracle

seemed to me to be a very serious man and an excellent choice for a marital relationship.

There you have it. I cannot state my frame of mind or my opinions at that time in my life more clearly. I did not know if I could even find him but I prayed everyday that someday me and Bobby could meet and get to know each other (and in the meantime I would concentrate on making myself a better and smarter person and do well in school) and up until the trouble happened I was doing excellent in school.

I wondered if dreams ever do really come true and if my deepest wishes could ever be fulfilled.

Life On the Road

Let's pick up the pieces of the Story Starting at Pecos.

I was about 10 miles out of town and with a trucker in the vastness of the desert. He pulled over and he got me down and raped me. I was very upset and I asked him why he'd done that to me. He replied, "Because you're a woman and that's what women are for !" I was very angry and when I got into town I called the sheriff's office to report him. The sheriff came and brought me to the hospital and got confirmation but told me that he could not just go chasing around looking for the trucker and that he'd be hard to find in those parts without a license plate number.

The sheriff brought me to Pecos Jail and that's where I met J.E. Couch who was a juvenile officer in Pecos. I was placed in a cell with two other juvenile girls (believe it when I tell you that they're names were Mary and Martha!) and

Ethel C. Richard

we spent a couple of days together talking, singing and reading the New Testament and teasing Jerry (who was the jailer in charge and used to bring our food and seemed to be a likable guy). The copy of the New Testament we had was called Good News for Man and was a modern translation that the Jesus Movement often turned to instead of the King James Version.

J.E. took me out of our cell one day and we had a talk together. I told him that I'd been heading to Tucson, Arizona to live at a Maranatha Christian Missionary House and that I could not go back to New Hampshire because there was too much trouble for me there. I gave to him the phone number to call and talk with Jack about it. He did call jack and together in a conference call I heard Jack tell him, "If you knew her parents you would understand why she is on the road."

It turned out that J.E. was a person who considered himself a "born again Christian" and so he called Tex (Clarence Young) who founded and operated the mission's house and we four continued with the conference. J.E. asked Tex what the house was all about and he asked Tex if he had been expecting to receive me there to live with them. Tex answered him, "She's welcome here as long as she loves the Lord!" That was all that J.E. needed to here. Within a day or so he gave to me some money and put me on a greyhound bus to Tucson. I called my Mom during a stop at El Paso while I was in route to Tucson on the bus and I told her that I was in route to Tucson and not to worry about me. She was upset and told me that the court was supposed to have returned me to New Hampshire and not send me to Tucson.

The Bobby Sherman Miracle

She said that an officer had called her and Dad, and those arrangements were being made to get the money to transport me back and so how could it be that the juvenile officer was sending me to Tucson?

I told her that she needed to understand that she'd been wrong to assume that I could not take care of myself and that he had emancipated me in letting me go. I spoke with her a few more minutes and told her to not upset herself because I would be perfectly alright. I hung up and got some food.

**REEVES COUNTY
SHERIFF'S DEPARTMENT
CORRECTIONAL BUILDING**
PHONE (915) 445-4901   FAX (915) 445-5405
POST OFFICE BOX 910
PECOS, TEXAS 79772

ARNULFO "ANDY" GOMEZ
SHERIFF
E. A. LUJAN
CHIEF DEPUTY

OCTOBER 17, 1995

TO WHOM IT MAY CONCERN:

RE: ETHEL RICHARDS W/F, DOB/061955,

THIS IS TO CERTIFY THAT THE ABOVE MENTIONED INDIVIDUAL WAS INCARCERATED AT THE REEVES COUNTY JAIL ON MAY 18, 1971 THRU MAY 25, 1971.

IF WE CAN BE OF FURTHER ASSISTANCE PLEASE FEEL FREE TO CONTACT US AT (915)445-4901.

SINCERELY,

HILDA WOODS, DEPUTY
REEVES COUNTY JAIL

SIGNED AND DATED THIS TUESDAY, OCTOBER 17, 1995

HILDA ANN WOODS, NOTARY
THE STATE OF TEXAS

Ethel C. Richard

Actually I say I was in route to Tucson but I was let off the bus in Phoenix and called the house from the bus station there. I was met in the Phoenix Greyhound Station by a close friend of Tex's wife Vera and escorted to a private home at which I stayed for a couple of nights. The family who I stayed with was very religious. The head of the family had a Christian radio show he did. It was nice because I finally got to sleep in a private room that had a nicely made twin bed and a bureau and they had a great breakfast ready in the morning! I ate a lot of pancakes and had orange juice and was happy.

The afternoon while I was there I threw on the radio and started dancing. I was stopped by the minister whose home it was and he told me that it would not be allowed because he could "see" what music did to me. (I'd been REALLY dancing because I enjoyed it and I had taught myself all of the popular moves). I had won dance contests which he would not have appreciated. Still, I was sad to go but I was going to be brought by car to Maranatha house and was very curiously wondering how things would be there.

I arrived at the house in Tucson and Vera showed me around. Jack was there in the back yard talking with some people. I suppose that Jack had left Manchester shortly after I had and had been waiting at the house for my arrival without my knowledge. This would mean that during our phone conference that Jack and Tex were both in the same location.

The house had a vegetable garden and that's the first thing I saw that I liked there. Jack showed to me an odd looking pepper and he told me to try it. I agreed and when I popped it into my mouth and chewed down on it I immediately

The Bobby Sherman Miracle

thought I would suffocate on the heat it produced. I had never had a hot pepper in my life before and I refused to admit that I was on fire. I chewed it up and swallowed it and all the while Jack was smiling at me with a wide smile on his face and after I'd finished he laughed as he asked me, "Well, how is it?!" I smiled back as sincerely as I could under the circumstances and I quipped, "…Good pepper!"

There were lots of people at the house both guys and ladies. They were mostly young people and from all parts of the United States. There was Pierre who had an accent and Mike who played guitar. Loupie (a Spanish girl I liked very much) and various others who I became friends with but since have forgotten their names. I shared a room with another couple of girls. I got to wear long (ankle length) dresses which I liked very much. I got to feel for a little while like part of a very large family and I enjoyed going to the co-op and getting food with them to bring back to the house for meals.

I liked cooking with the girls and the nightly bible studies that were headed by Tex. On Sundays we went to church. In the afternoons we would get into a homemade auto (a dune buggy) and drive into parts of Tucson and witness to strangers we met in the streets about the love of God for people and recite scripture to those who would listen. We invited people to let Jesus become the Lord of their life and to ask him into their hearts. "Have you accepted Jesus?" we would ask… "For God so loved the world that he gave his only begotten son, that whosoever believeth on him should not perish but should have everlasting life!"

Ethel C. Richard

Many persons would stop and listen to us and take our literature home with them and many wondered why young people would be preaching God's love for them out in the streets instead of being out partying at other kinds of functions. Everything was cool for a short while when I first moved into the house but then after about a week something odd was in the air and I did not like the feel of it.

I had run into a man who lived across the street from the house and we'd talked a little bit. He kissed me (I was not very impressed by him) and Tex and Vera caught wind of it. They were upset and told me that I could not talk with the guy who lived next door. They said that since he was not a Christian I was forbidden to talk with him. I agreed and that should have been the end of it.

Instead, Vera within a day or two called me into a room with the woman who had brought me to the house from Phoenix and tried to counsel me about an institution in Arizona called Camelback Girls Residence. She told me that they were trying to get me admitted to that institution because I should be with girls my own age and in a regular kid's home environment. I knew something was amiss and I started to suspect trouble. Toward the end of the week Vera informed me that Camelback had refused my admission because the paperwork had to be done by a legal guardian or a parent. I sensed they were uneasy because they did not have legal custody of me and were afraid that police might get involved at my being there. I began to get that feeling of uncertainty and insecurity that I'd felt on the road.

The following Sunday after we'd all left church Vera and

The Bobby Sherman Miracle

Tex put me inside of their car and we drove to an elderly couple's home. When we got inside there appeared to be only the man and his wife there. They seemed very nice and the man's wife offered me some banana bread and I ate it. Then suddenly my left arm was grabbed securely by Tex and I was put on the floor forcibly by the two men and many other people were suddenly there and all touching me while I was being held forcibly face and stomach down onto the carpet. What followed was a complete disrespect for common sense and a terrible assault which I was under an obligation to somehow create a way out of the suffocating situation.

Tex's idea of ridding himself of a disturbing problem was to assume that the devil had everything to do with it and so therefore he felt that it was his personal duty before God to perform a Christian exorcism.

I knew I was in for quite a rough ride after they would not let me up off the floor. (These guys were really pushing on me and hurting me). They kept asking some imaginary demon what his name was and insisting like a bunch of maniacs. I had to make up about 50 different names of demons and behave like a crazed person (growling and making up stories) just to get them all to get the hell off of me…!

When it was all finally over I was so exhausted that I nearly could not get up off the carpet. When I did, I did not peep even a syllable but kept to myself. We went back to the house with Tex and Vera who was touting the "most successful exorcism ever" and the next morning me and Jack were standing in front of the house together when he looked long and hard at me and asked me, "You are leaving aren't you?"

Ethel C. Richard

I looked toward the road and then I looked him straight in the eye and I said very seriously, "Yeah...." and with my hands in my pockets I shuffled my feet in determination to leave Maranatha far, far behind me. That was the last time I saw Jack until late 1971 (back in Manchester while I was on a home visit with my parents during my second hospital stay). I never said goodbye to Tex and Vera or anyone else there. Only Jack knew that I was going back on the road.

November 3, 1994

Ms Ethel "CeeCee" Richards

Dear CeeCee,

We certainly were suprised when you called the other day to hear from you after 25 years. I remember when you were in the Maranatha House for about three weeks in May or June of 1971.

Maranatha House was a live-in discipleship ministry to new Christians, that we started in August of 1970. Jack Motin was the first person from New Hampshire and then Raymond Coutu. They were at the Maranatha House for several months. Three years later John Fortin joined us and helped in the ministry for about two years.
We saw many people set free from drugs and find a meaningful life through faith in our Lord Jesus Christ in the six years of Maranatha House ministry.

We would encourage you, as we do everyone, to let Jesus be the Lord of your life. Only in Him do we find life, peace and joy.

In His Service,

C.R. & Vera Young

The Bobby Sherman Miracle

Ethel is fifth from the left (bottom row and center front) behind Jack Morin with pointed finger who kneels directly between the two men sitting cross legged at the front.

Jack realized that what had happened there had made me very apprehensive about Tex and Vera. He knew I was not abnormal or demon possessed. He knew that they were becoming fanatic and had done wrong to me by jumping me physically at the pastor's house. I realized that the House of Maranatha for me was history.

I set my sights on Burbank, California remembering my original idea back in Manchester (and which idea I'd held onto secretly...) which was my determined desire and quest to find and meet Bobby Sherman.

Chapter Ten

"Bobby Sherman, Here I come…"
Ethyle' Gets Together with Bobby Sherman

I made fast travel to Los Angeles from Tucson getting to Los Angeles somewhere around the end of first or second week of June 1971. I stayed in central LA for a night and then I picked up a copy of Tiger Beat Magazine and noted the address of its editorial offices and hitched a ride to go have a talk with Anne Moses who knew everything it seemed about Bobby and who I was sure could tell me where to find him. Anne was a wonderful lady and took me into her office right away upon my arrival.

We sat down together and I explained to her that I was from New Hampshire and had come a very long way with the idea in mind to meet Bobby Sherman. She looked at me and smiled brightly and exclaimed, "That's great…! Whew! For a minute I was worried you were going to say David Cassidy, and he's not very easy to meet (but Bobby is a really great guy

Ethel C. Richard

and he is VERY EASY to meet!"

I beamed with happiness and excitement at her words.

She spent the following minutes giving me precise directions to the Columbia Screen Gems TV Studios Ranch and writing them down for me. She told me that it was at the corner of Oak Street and Hollywood Way in Burbank and she also told me what date that Bobby would be starting work there on his new show and she even told me what time of day to be there and to wait for him to drive into the driveway of the ranch very early in the morning (before seven am). I thanked Anne wholeheartedly (while inside I thanked God too) and I left knowing that I would finally meet Bobby at the ranch the following week. It was all I could do to keep from jumping up and down. I was very happy.

I kicked around LA for a few days longer until the morning of the date that Anne had given me.

I was at the driveway of the studios at six am and waiting and boy was I ever nervous! I spent the whole time praying for a miracle that everything would somehow work out alright between I and Bobby. I wanted for him to like me and I wanted to make an impression on him so that I would be in his thoughts and be able to see him again after our first meeting. I did not have really cool clothes or makeup and so I would have to find some other way than looking absolutely gorgeous in order to grab his attention.

Not that I was anything but cute and had a perfect hourglass figure but there's only so much that can be done with a baggy shirt and jeans which were all the clothes I owned (My dad's long sleeve dark brown shirt and baggy bells that were embroidered "keep on truckin'" on the pants leg) and I had to go dressed in clothes…you know? So I would have to come up with something different and catchy to grab Bobby's notice.

I decided to tell him my name the way my Dad had always pronounced it. Like I told you before, Dad was a true Frenchman and he always used a French accent…so I would tell Bobby my name was, Ethyle' with a French roll of the tongue (Eat- el) and also try to get his attention in whatever way would present itself to me when I saw him.

I saw his truck drive up just as he came around the corner and I jumped right up off the curb - and making a running jump, I blocked his path (waving my arms in the air frantically) and was directly in front of him flagging him and exclaiming, "Bobby, Bobby please stop…!" (If he had not stopped I would have been run over because I would never have moved away)….!

Bobby did stop and he was startled from my sudden appearance out of nowhere. He had a nice smile on his face and his first words to me were, "Ok, kiss me baby." He tilted his head toward me (cheek first) while pointing his finger to his cheek. I very slowly and very soulfully brushed his ear at his hairline with my lips caressing his left cheek and the edge of his mouth in a very meaningful slow and easy with my lips the entire length of his face while snuggling my nose into his skin and inhaling deeply.

You know the kind of kiss I mean…done right they are more like a warm snuggle and a deep drinking in of the other person's essence and natural breath, transforming a kiss into an moment like when appreciating a fine gourmet wine (delicacy) and I was savoring in the moment that I wanted to last forever!

Bobby asked me my name and I said to him, "My name is, Ethyle'"

"You have very unusual name. How do I spell that?" he said, as he took a large pink post-it notepad from his dash and wrote me note which read, "Ethyle', I love you, Baby!" Then signed it... *Bobby.*

He had to go inside and so I hung around asking God to get me inside the studios to be near him.

While I was hanging around on the curb within the driveway a man came up to me out of nowhere and sat down beside me. He said his name was Ruben and he asked me if I would like to go inside the facility. Well of course I said sure. He took me to a utility building close by and he showed me a way inside and told me where inside to go to find set 29. He told me that was where Bobby was working and he added, "Just act like you belong there and everybody will believe that you do belong there."

Now I guess it should have occurred to me as odd that a strange man with shoulder length hair showed up suddenly out of nowhere and magically knows that I am there to visit with Bobby and gets me inside the sets after I had just met Bobby fifteen minutes earlier.... and then tells me precisely where to go to find the set where he is working and how to behave while I am there...

I did not think about it then as unusual but since then I have come to a conclusion that Bobby knew that guy (Ruben)

The Bobby Sherman Miracle

and that he told him to look for me at the front of the place and to show me inside.

It would not have been the only time that Bobby sent others on an errand to talk with me or to give to me something. Doing that seemed to be Bobby's habit when he was working. He bought for me a large sandwich and a soda and had Wes hand it to me while he went to the front of the bleachers because he was waiting for a scene to start. I remember leaving my seat and walking up to him (I was kidding around and trying to be clever) and holding my cigarette I asked him sarcastically if he had a "good match" (meaning "can we get matched up together?") Bobby scolded me saying, "Forget your cigarette. Sit down and eat!"

He had been preoccupied in thought and so he was not in the mood for dumb behavior from me. He sent Wes to me with a message occasionally like when Wes put money into my hand and told me, "This is from Bobby. He says, "Hurry…they are coming for you. Call your mother and tell her you're alright." I did not know who Wes was (truly) and so I asked his name. He looked at me jokingly and said, "I am the OTHER Bobby….!"

Ethel C. Richard

*Photo of Wesley Stern and Bobby Sherman.
From 'Getting Together' days in 1971...*

I am sure he meant that he was the other star of the show and he probably thought that I was weird because I had no clue about what show was being filmed or who he was...!

More recently I have had other memories surface of being with Bobby that I had not remembered for years and I am exploring where they took place and what they mean. I know that they are memories and not my imagination because of the crystal clarity of the events and situations in them. For instance, I would have no logical reason to envision Bobby sitting very closely together with me on a wooden bench while sitting at a table inside a small office and he wearing dark grey knit and slim exercise pants with a two tone

The Bobby Sherman Miracle

matching knit jacket with light grey color panels on its sleeves and in sneakers.

To my recollection I have never in my life seen a picture of Bobby wearing such a getup.

In this memory I can actually feel the hardness of the bench (which is dark brown) and I am leaning over with my elbows on the table and I have a small piece of white paper under my right hand and a pen and Bobby is telling me to write some information on the paper. He wants to know my mother's name and her phone number. He is very kind and soft spoken and he tells me, "I do not want you to do that…" (And I know he means he does not want for me to hitchhike).

In this memory we are together for quite some time and he is talking very gently with me and is concerned about me. He has his arm around my right shoulder and I am looking closely, directly into his face as he speaks with me. We are sitting so close together that our thighs are touching and I cannot possibly mistake who he is because I am watching closely his face as he speaks. I can remember what he said and how my feelings were jumping all over the place while he spoke. I was very quiet and simply listened to him. I remember he got up after a while to leave and he gave me a kiss and told me to be good.

There is another person in the room too. She is a dark haired woman who is waiting. Observing this memory I get the impression that she is Joan Hancack. (Joan Hancack, I remember she was my Los Angeles, California probation officer upon my third incident of being taken into custody in Burbank and who had given to me Bobby's message). There is

Ethel C. Richard

something very odd about this scene in that Joan would not have been looking to find out my parents information during my second stay at juvenile hall in Burbank because the court at Burbank had already known me and had sent me back to Manchester a time before.

And Joan was not my probation officer at the time of what I'd believed was my first stay at the juvenile hall during June. The proof of this is in the court papers themselves which name a different probation officer in my case for June. The June papers state that I was in custody in Los Angeles in June and was being returned to Manchester. The later dated papers state that Joan is my PO and that am being returned to Manchester (the later papers are dated September 2, 1971) and there is scheduled an additional hearing set for a non appearance calendar of March 1972.

Adding to my confusion is the fact of my parents address listed within the documents does not jive within my memory of what really happened after I'd first been sent home to Manchester from Los Angeles. I got off the plane at Manchester Airport and my dad and mom put me into dad's car and we drove back to our apartment on Fourth Street. That's when my dad had told me to "Shut Up" because I was talking about Bobby while on the ride home. (How could our address in the court papers be Lake Avenue when I had been sent back to my parents who lived on Fourth Street)?

Because of this new memory I got I decided to go back to the papers and examine them more closely.

The State Hospital record reads that I had run away from home three times and not two as I'd believed.

The Bobby Sherman Miracle

This floored me because I had not known I'd run away three times. I know for fact that I had met Bobby before my return to *Fourth Street*. (But the two sets of papers I have from the Los Angeles courts do not even list the Fourth Street address). It's as if they'd never heard of it. I know I was with Bobby on his birthday on July 22 and July through August is not even acknowledged in the paperwork.

This is where things get complicated. I believe that I'd only been at House of Maranatha no more than two weeks (Pecos Jail document states that I was incarcerated there up through May 25th which adding one day for the bus ride would put me at Maranatha through maybe Monday June 7th (right after I'd had the bad experience with Tex and Vera at the elderly couples home on that previous Sunday) and so that gave me plenty of time to hitch a ride out to Los Angeles and have my meeting with Anne Moses and still have a few days left before Bobby's show was scheduled to begin filming.

By the process of deduction I have come to the conclusion that Bobby's first day of work on his show must have been early enough during June that there was time for me to meet Bobby and be taken into custody and sent back to Manchester within a week of being taken into custody again at Burbank, Los Angeles on June 22.

I know that I was sent home to Fourth Street and during the ride home in the car from the airport my dad had spoken roughly with me and I ran away again immediately upon my first chance the following day. This would put me back in Burbank in plenty of time to be taken into custody again at the studios June 22.

Ethel C. Richard

I have begun to believe that there may have been a meeting between my probation officer Joan Hancack and me somewhere between June 8th and June 11th and that she did not know where to find my folks and had called Bobby in realizing that I would not cooperate if he did not talk with me and ask me to cooperate. I know that I babbled at the mouth constantly about having been there at the Columbia Screen Gems Ranch with him and that I did not want him to think I'd just disappeared.

I bugged the officers to tell Bobby where I was and that I was ok. I think they contacted him and asked him to please come down to the station. Hence the strange dream of a memory sitting with Bobby at the table on a bench in an office with Joan Hancack present in the room.

I have no other explanation for this memory that would even make any sense to me. The things he had said to me had meant so much to me and yet could it be that I had forgotten that he'd been there with me in the office with Joan Hancack and had helped her to get me to give to them information of who were my parents? But how can it have happened this way I ask myself. For forty three years I had remembered something entirely different from this dream scenario of Bobby sitting with me and trying to get me to tell the officer on paper my mother's telephone phone number or address.

I had remembered only that Joan Hancack had told me within a couple of days of my being taken into custody that she had contacted Bobby and that he had told her that he "meets a lot of girls" (but that he had given to her a message to relay to me of what he wanted me to do...which was, "Go home, be

The Bobby Sherman Miracle

good, get a job and save your money and then when you turn eighteen years old, Come Back!" (She'd put extra stress on the last two words of his message, making it clear that she knew he'd actually remembered who I was and intended that his message be delivered in that way). I now believe that it's possible that this message was delivered to me the third and last time I'd been taken into custody in Burbank.

I believe that Bobby was covering for himself when he'd told her that he "meets a lot of girls" before passing his message to relay to me. I know that Bobby would do that (because he had to consider his image in his career and to have known a runaway girl of sixteen years old maybe would have created an image problem (as well as other problems) for him.

That was my memory of it... (my only memory of it) until the memory dream of that small office and a private talk with Bobby (and Joan Hancack who was in the office with us) and sitting with him on a bench at a small square or slightly rectangular table surfaced in my mind. I'd gone to sleep and I'd had the dream one night about it (unexpectedly) while I have been trying to remember things while writing this book of my auto-biography.

This would make sense because in the June 22 document (which does not have the Fourth Street address but my parents having moved during my second runaway travels, it lists the Lake Avenue address) it lists a deputy assistant PO name and not that of Joan Hancack which may indicate that though Joan was my PO she had an assistant working on my case after being taken into custody the second time..

As for my strange and very detailed real seeming dream, I

Ethel C. Richard

think that I and Bobby were together in that office and sitting at that bench. I say this because after I'd returned to Burbank the second time when Bobby saw me waiting for him again in the driveway of the studios he was very surprised. So surprised that he literally jumped onto his shift with a sudden jerk and exclaimed, "You're back...!"

It was obvious to me that day that he knew who I was and that I'd been taken into custody prior to that meeting with him. It was too obvious that he was aware of me and that he had recognized me immediately. He also was very happy to actually see me again and I was ecstatic to see his face again as well. I exclaimed to him, "You didn't think I'd stay away that long did you Bobby?!"

He jumped out of his pickup truck...small and sunny yellow with an emblem on the front grill (VW?) and we stood together for photos (my girlfriend took the pictures) in front of his open truck door with our arms around each other's waists.

I believe that the morning Bobby saw me and exclaimed "You're back...!" took place after I'd run away the second time. Hence the court record of having been taken into custody on June 22 (after having visited with Bobby for the day). The time of day listed on the document does not match up to the time of day that I was taken into custody the third time in Burbank (which was after 8 pm) at my girlfriend's house within a block or so from the studios.

The time of day on June 22 that I was taken into custody was 5:20 pm and I'd been with Bobby and an actress whose name was Cindy the entire day.

The Bobby Sherman Miracle

I'd visited with Cindy Williams in her trailer that morning just talking and when she asked if I'd like a cookie I ate every one of her new box of Entenmann's Hermit Cookies...

I hadn't eaten in days and I was really hungry. Later Bobby showed up at Cindy's trailer looking for me so that we could talk and about an hour later he had bought me lunch of a huge whopper sandwich, fries and a large soda....

I sat around with others on a bleachers bench just hanging out and listening to the music (the Getting Together recording was played) and watching Bob and the other actors and paying attention to what they were doing. That day was very unique and I was very happy to be near Bobby, Cindy and Wes.

Everything felt good and right and natural. I had fun.

Ethel C. Richard

I am not positive however I think that was the day when Bobby sent Wes over to me while I was sitting in the park to give me some money to call my mom and to warn me that they were coming for me so that I could quickly get out of there and not get caught. But I was in such a daze that I did not comprehend that I actually had to leave the studio driveway. I didn't want to go. I got taken into custody by Burbank police on Screen Gems property because I was dumb and did not listen to Bobby when he sent me the message to leave and call my mom. I guess that once I'd stared into Bobby's blue eyes and face to face (he'd kissed me earlier in the day while holding my shoulders within his hands while I'd stared into his face studying him) and I was hypnotized!

So that's where the police found me. In the driveway sitting on the curb at the entrance to the Columbia Screen Gems Ranch after just having been sitting and visiting with Bobby in the park inside the facility (and having just a few moments before been talking with Wes who had delivered to me Bobby's message to leave and to call my mother with the money he'd sent with Wes to give to me - which Wesley had done. He'd put the money directly into my left hand).

So to make a more complicated story shorter I was taken into custody again and brought to LA Central Juvenile Hall. I was sent back to Manchester again, this time I went with my folks from the airport to Lake Avenue.

My stay with mom and dad didn't last long because I did it again…. I ran next day. (Third time)

I literally just remembered this (as I am sitting here today

The Bobby Sherman Miracle

at my computer and writing) and I am shaking my head in disbelief that I just got up and took off to the highway after just a few hours sitting at our kitchen table. I just could not sit still and stay there waiting for court (I'd been told by mom court was going to happen in a few days) All that mattered to me and I wanted was to be with Bobby and I had no intention of staying.

The next time I saw Bobby was on his birthday (July 22). I gave to him a kiss (he always asked me for a kiss) and I gave to him a cute birthday card I'd picked up at a store down the street from the ranch. Bobby must have been beside himself wondering, *what the hell is going on with this girl?*

There was a cute message on the card something like, "What you should get for your birthday is me!" and signed, Ethyle.' When I came back later that day the person at the gate said that Bobby had left for the day. I was leaving the ranch driveway when a small white mobile studio truck stopped and the driver asked me if I wanted a ride.

He was also coming out from the studios ranch and so I said sure and jumped into the cab. We went to his place (a flat somewhere in LA) and drank 7 UP for hours while we talked and I watched him draw Flintstone cartoon characters onto large pieces of transparent film. He explained the cartoon making process and we had a great time just sitting around and talking. I think I was back at the ranch the following morning but my memory gets hazy here. I remember the man's face (thin) and that he appeared to be in his early thirties and was of slim build and taller than Bobby but I do not remember his name. He was very nice to invite

Ethel C. Richard

me to stay with him at his flat and it turned out to be a fun time for me. (I was very interested in cartoon animation). That's all that took place that night. He lived alone and so I and he simply shared some nice company while talking and drinking 7UP.

Some memories that I have of Bobby and me together are a bit jumbled because to me they do not make sense unless we'd had more than just a small chat together about small stuff. I will share them with you here however keep in mind that I have no explanation for the circumstance of these bits and pieces of memory other than the fact that I have them and even I make it a point to not attach too much to them. There is a memory I have of Bobby and me in a room where there is a bed and he is in stocking feet (dark blue or black socks) and he is thinking and is upset and refusing to accept something that's happened though I do not remember what has happened.

I also have a memory of looking up into Bobby's face from a position such as when your head's on someone's lap and you are both in a vehicle and you are looking up straight into his face while he is driving. (I did not say that this makes any sense). I remember being in an office room with Bobby as well...and the reason Bobby was there with me was to get me to remember my folks address because nobody knew where my folks were.

In this memory Bobby and me are sitting closely together on a dark bench (our thighs touching) at a small rectangular or square dark table (both the table and the bench were close to the wall and he had his arm around my shoulder and

The Bobby Sherman Miracle

hugging my neck and was talking softly with me and telling me that he did not want me to hitchhike anymore at all and that he cared about what happened with me and that it was important that Joan have my parents address. All of this conversation (which was Bobby doing the talking with me and me not saying anything... as I remember being very, very quietly listening to what he said to me) and all the while my Los Angeles probation officer Joan Hancack was in the room standing off in a corner near to the secretaries window and was watching us.

This memory is spooky to me because I can remember even how our thighs were touching together while we sat on that bench and I remember what Bobby was wearing and how softly he spoke with me and gently explained to me his thoughts. He wore a matching very casual grey pant and soft knit two tone jersey type long sleeve. His pants were not the corderoy that I'd seen him wear before at the ranch when he'd first come into work mornings. These were different and were more like expensive knit exercise wear (soft and comfortable).

We'd had other talks while we were visiting together at the ranch (like when I'd told him what had happened to me at Pecos [I'd been raped and had called the sheriff to hunt down the guy and put him in jail for statutory] and after tests [the sheriff took me to a doctor] the guy had gotten away and I'd been put in jail for a week till the Pecos juvenile officer JE Couch figured out what to do with me...and then he decided to release me... putting me onto a greyhound bus to Tex and Vera Young who founded The House of Maranatha at Tucson, Arizona). So, Bobby and me talked about this and

Ethel C. Richard

more than this and not just about cheeseburgers and so I would have thought of myself as (at the very least) a friend and certainly more than a mere acquaintance given the circumstances.

The last day ever I was with Bobby was very sad for me. I'd left him for a little while to visit with my girlfriend at her house while he was working. (She was a young girl who used to like hanging around in the driveway on the curb with her camera and take photos of celebrities who came in and out of the ranch). I remember she liked David Cassidy. She understood I was hangin' with Bobby. I've forgotten her name but I am trying to find her and if she should read this book I hope she will come to me and we can talk. I also hope that she kept the pictures of me and Bobby that she took while we were visiting at the studios. I returned to Bobby later that day around lunchtime but he had already left to get food and so I and my girlfriend waited sitting on the curb till we saw him come in.

He was passenger in the back seat of a car… a light color blue two tone with what looked like grey or silver sedan. (Not the Rolls) Caddy and I think and I don't fully remember who was driving. (I did not really pay attention to who was driving) but I think it was Wes. I walked up to the car wearing a really short pair of paisley hot pants and a tiny thin yellow cotton short waist scoop T shirt that had a small flower embroidery or emblem at the mid breast point and I wore no brazier because quite frankly I did not own one.

Wes stopped the car and I stood at the passenger window and leaned fully into the car and I asked him if we could meet at four o'clock. He said yes and so I stood up straight and turned to walk away from the car took a few steps and then I turned to look back and watch the car drive into the gate but the car was still not moving. Bobby was standing upright with his entire torso out of the window of the car and staring at me with his eyes popped and the way he was looking at me made me feel really frazzled and hot and unable to move. He had the biggest smile I've ever seen (teeth showing and ear to ear).

It was obvious that he liked my body in the little shirt and shorts and I just stood there blushing and unable to move. I stared right back and I wished someone would have kicked me out of my fear. Bobby had wanted me to come back to the car so that he could talk with me and all I could do was freeze.

He got slowly back down into the car and the car moved slowly into the main parking area.

Has anyone reading this seen the movie Sleepless in Seattle? The part where Annie is standing in the road and almost gets hit by a Mack truck because she is staring at Sam and then she and Sam finally get to stare into each other's eyes from across the road…and all she could say was, "Hello." And he also says, "Hello"? Annie feels so embarrassed that she turns away and goes back home to Baltimore in a frazzle. I felt exactly like that. I had asked him to meet me at around 4 pm and then BAM …!!!

I turned to watch the car pull away and I instead got "hit "(psychology run right over me) by the Mack Truck whose name is Bobby Sherman. (Bobby's was staring directly at my body with his eyes ogling me and with his mouth gaping

Ethel C. Richard

open)...! That's what happened. It was just exactly like that. He looked very puzzled after staying there for some time and waiting for me to approach him.

I turned and walked away (so bashful that I was totally mortified) and I do not know for sure if I ever saw him again after that. I think that it was the last time I'd seen him and I am still beside myself with grief that I'd completely frozen in fear.

Just an interesting note: I ran across a statement in a legal jargon book of information and statistics having to deal with girls incarcerated within facilities in America and which includes this statement, "Non delinquent reasons accounted for 20 percent of girls being held in juvenile detention facilities in 1989. The most common non delinquent reason for confinement was a status offence. More than 75 percent of female juveniles in public facilities for non delinquent reasons had committed status offenses such as running away, truancy and incorrigibility." *From the book Female Crime, Criminals and Cellmates by Ronald Barri Flowers, published 1995 by McFarland.*

Being sixteen years old and from Manchester, New Hampshire during my 1971 trek I certainly could not be called truant from school because a kid from New Hampshire could legally quit school at sixteen years. So, what's left is that I was very independent and on my own. I had always minded my own business in Manchester and when I did run into problems with the neighborhood gangs I had reported such to either school authorities or police and my parents. I had reported to my father what his brother had done. In no case were my complaints taken seriously.

I was not seeking trouble. I was not promiscuous and I wanted to stay in school and even earn a scholarship which was within my reach though my family was very monetarily poor. The same was true while I was traveling throughout the United States as a sixteen year old. I totally avoided sexual confrontations. I was at times in very dangerous and seemingly inescapable and risky situations and most times I was able with my wits to get away. There were a few times when the only escape was to play along until I could find escape. Such a thing did happen.

I'd hitched a ride and the man it turned out was a criminal who molested me and beat me and told me that he was keeping me to sell me to someone who was running a sex slave ring. I played along telling him that "Ok, I could use a place to stay and some nice clothes and cash…" (ad nauseum) … and he bought into it. He stopped at a small combination gas station and grocer to get gas and cigarettes and parked quite a distance from the store entrance.

I saw what might be my only chance for escape and I unlocked the door of the van and booked it fast as I could across the lot and into the store and ran behind the counter begging the clerk to please help me escape that man because he had beat me and made me do things and was planning on selling me. I stood behind the counter with the owner of the store and when the man came inside he said to me, "So, you decided to turn me in, huh?"

Ethel C. Richard

"Get the hell out of here," I answered. "I don't ever want to see you again. I called the cops and they're on their way!"

He left and the police were taking forever to show up. I decided it might be best if I just moved along out of there and I got a ride. I knew that a real bad guy got away and I hope he did not go out and hurt another girl ... but at the time I had to think fast and I hated him and wanted him gone. I breathed a sigh of relief when the sight of his van was long gone.

Upon another time (I think I was traveling through Tennessee somewhere just outside Knoxville) I'd just jumped out of an eighteen wheeler which had stopped in a breakdown lane and whose driver had me worrying about his intentions. It was late evening and I did not see the exit ramp nearby within 300 feet of the truck until next morning.

I got scared and I ran off the highway and straight into a very high barbed wire chain link fence. The fence was about three times my height with an added three or four section of barbed wire. I was panic driven and seeing no way out I climbed the fence and threw myself over it with all my strength. This was not a small feat for a very petite young girl. I got caught by my pant ankle in the barbs on the way down and hung upside down for a while as I tried to solve my problem. I was extremely exhausted and struggling to stay awake and realizing that I was caught and could not stay upside down I (using all of my energy) reached toward my pant cuff and I gave a quick jerk to the cloth material as I fell to the ground.

I righted myself and seeing a hotel in the distance I

walked the way straightest to get to it through a field of grass which was overgrown and taller than I was by a few inches. I got to the hotel and walked in the front door in a horrible state and I asked the clerk behind the desk if he had a spot to clean up and rest and he put a room key in front of me and told me to be out by 6 am. Truthfully I believe he saw me run from the truck, climb the fence and get caught upside down, free myself and run/walk through the high grasses to get to the hotel door). He gave to me a knowing look as he put the key down on the counter.

I am still VERY grateful to that very charitable hotel desk clerk.

It's time I sew up the actual facts of what happened at Denver, Colorado and of why I was so terribly against police after the incidents there.

I arrived in lower downtown Denver somewhere around nine pm on a rainy night and I saw the Denver police station sign and was so very tired that I walked into the station and asked the officer manning the front desk if he would allow me to just sit in one of the chairs and get out of the rain and rest for the night. He looked at me and told me that he could not allow me to stay within the station but that he would get me a ride to a place where I would be safe and to wait until he had a car ready.

I was ushered into the back seat of a Denver police car and two officers drove me to St. Andrew's Episcopal Church at 2015 Glenarm Place and pointing to the crypt door the officer driving said to me, "You see that big door at the side? Open that door and go inside. You will be safe here."

Ethel C. Richard

Having no reason to question what the officer had said I thanked him for the ride and I did as he told me. It was very dark inside but within a moment or so of my going inside I heard a male voice.... "Hey man, it's a chick!" Someone suddenly grabbed me and I was thrown around. I knew that I was being raped and things became a blur.

Since I have already written a piece about what happened at Denver I am including it here mainly because what happened at Denver is still difficult for me to write about and I want to avoid too much emotional stress as I relate these events.

Chapter Eleven

A Brief Synopsis

I had lost the memory of many years of my life to forced drugging and electric shock which was imposed upon me while I was an inpatient at N.H. State Hospital from January 1970 to April 1971 and then again from Sept 1971 through December 1971. I had never had seizures and Tardive Dyskinesia before I was hospitalized. I was discharged from the hospital suffering from both and I always felt like I was in a terrible fog. I for a long time had dull senses and dull emotions and I felt different from others and very alone.

My voice had an odd hollow echo to me and I felt as if I were someone else. I had a sensation of being out of my body (disassociated) much of the time. I had very severe memory loss and I had strange nightmares. I could not think clearly or be alert. I had (and still do have) dexterity problems and constant ringing in my ears. My vision is scrambled in my right eye. I became partially deaf and I had balance and gait difficulties. These are known adverse neurological effects of psychotropic medications and electric shock. My jaw was out of line and my teeth shifted. (This most likely was caused from the many times I had received facial fractures). By the

Ethel C. Richard

time I was 32 years old my teeth had been removed because they had been shifting and had developed terrible infection. Many of these things over the years I have learned to either live with or reasonably subdue.

Since my memories began to surface (which started in early 1994) I had developed an additional problem with short term memory lapses which scared me. I would set out to go somewhere and totally forget how to get there. I would buy food at a fast food place and drive away without the food and only remember after I got home. I am having much fewer of these episodes today. Through a lot of determination I work to stay aware, alert. I fight this problem with diet and getting enough rest and exercise. I have insulin dependent diabetes. Despite all this I am today stable and reasonably happy. However writing about the subject of my past can be a little trying. Thankfully it only bothers me when I am purposely trying to remember it.

I have not taken any drugs stronger than Advil in over 30 years and no alcohol in over 21 years. I credit this as the reason my brain has been able to some extent heal itself and why a lot of my memory from those years has returned. However, I have only a very few memories from the New Hampshire State Hospital.

I have no memory whatsoever of the coma and of being in the hospital in Denver where I had been admitted into St. Luke's Medical Center after again having been attacked by other criminals which incident happened at St. Andrew's Episcopal Church (lower downtown) approximately July 1, 1971.

The Bobby Sherman Miracle

Note for the record: After 3 days in the hospital and then another perhaps 4 days in Denver I followed my friend Rodney to Tillamook, Oregon (he was 17) after he was arrested by Denver police right in front of me, to pay him back his money because he emptied out his pockets of money to help me when he was arrested.

Amazing (isn't it?) how Rodney was arrested by Denver police right in front of me...

And while we were together on the sidewalk near the church, yet they REFUSED to take me into custody! (?)

I was only 16 years old and a girl who'd been hospitalized after being attacked and left for dead at the church and the police knew I was a minor because the hospital notified the police that I had been attacked there. The Denver Police Department even notified my parents that I was hospitalized in Denver after having been poisoned and raped. These facts leave a lot of questions unanswered and raise more than a few eyebrows.

The history of the Denver police raid of St. Andrews proves that Denver police knew I was there and that they had planned the raid because of me and other minors being there. The real question should be, could they not know? And why would they leave me and all other minors at the church alone with such hardened criminals, killers, military escapees, robbers and dangerous drugs and guns being hidden there?

The truth is frightening even to this day. I had gone to the

Ethel C. Richard

police for help when I'd first arrived in Denver. It was the police who brought me to the crypt of the church in the evening hours and told me to open the door and go inside and that I would be safe there. I was immediately attacked and gang raped by the group of men staying in the crypt and then kept prisoner by one of the brothers of the order upstairs in the adjacent building. When I got loose and could not remember what had happened to me there, the police arrested Rodney to separate us because he had been hanging with me there to protect me after I got out of the hospital. They hadn't figured that I would leave town to return to him his cash.

After approximately two weeks in Tillamook I was escorted out of town by the sheriff's deputy and let off in Lincoln City, Oregon. I from there traveled south to Bobby in Burbank at the ranch. (End of note)

The letter from Rod Lukens has always been very hard for me to take. It's a little graphic and I never get used to it. It is very embarrassing and I am more than deeply upset by it. I have included it here. I was going to type it so that the words would be easier to read but I just start crying so much and I get a very nauseated feeling when I read it so I scanned it instead.

To add a few more facts into this huge mess is that I had at first when I arrived in Denver gone to the police department and begged the officer at the front desk to please allow me to stay there in the police station and rest for the night in a chair. It was the police who told me that no, I could not be allowed to stay inside the police station but that they would bring me to a safe place where they knew was safe and I could stay.

The Bobby Sherman Miracle

I was put in a police car and delivered to St. Andrew's Episcopal Church. When the officer stopped the car he pointed at the door to the crypt of the church and told me "go open that door and go inside and you can sleep there. It is safe there." I did as he told me and I was attacked by a group of men a few moments later. I was also held prisoner at St. Andrew's Episcopal Church in a room upstairs and repeatedly assaulted by a black brother of the church.

I do remember his face. I also remember the head rector. His name was Stark. He had a limp. He took me into his office and was very angry and demanded that I GO AWAY. I believe that this happened after I was referred back to the church because it had a food kitchen and I did not remember what had happened to me there. So I walked right back into the same problem. I stayed. I was poisoned by strychnine within a couple of days. Rod helped me to stay alive that night. I and Rod believed they were trying to kill me. I left Denver to bring Rod his money which he gave to me when he was arrested. He told me his hometown name and I told him I would see him there. I did meet him later in Tillamook.

I did not remember Denver. I was harassed in Tillamook by the sheriff who came to my hotel room one day and told me to get out of town by 3 pm. When I laughed in his face and asked him if he thought that he 'is living in a John Wayne movie....?." he had his deputy stop me in front of the hotel with the police car at around 4 pm and he really scared me. The deputy yelled at me and demanded that I get into his car... He yelled, "NOW! THERE IS A MAN WITH A GUN AROUND THE CORNER WHO WANTS YOU

Ethel C. Richard

DEAD...Hurry up. Get in Now!"

I got into his car fast. He told me that he was bringing me to Lincoln City where I would be safe. I begged him to help me get a message to Rod so he drove me to Rod's house just long enough to tell him I was leaving town. I asked the deputy, "what do I tell Rod? "and he replied, "tell him you're going to a party in Lincoln City." The sheriff's deputy had very curly hair. His name was Dave Wilson. All of this is the absolute truth. I would swear on a stack of Bibles. I still sometimes cry uncontrollably because Denver and Tillamook are very hard for me to deal with emotionally.

Evidence

Rodney's Letter

Dear Ethel,   11-14-95

    I'll try to remember as much about Dracula that I can.
    I don't know if you arrived at the church before or after I did. The first time I saw you was in St Luke's Hospital. Some other kids and I went to see you after we heard what had happened to you. We didn't know you then, but most everyone at the church was hurt.
    When I first heard about it, I was in the sanctuary in front of the church. A group of guys were talking about how they had gotten a girl all messed up and were taking turns with her. The only one in the bunch I knew was the blond heavy set brother of the church. He used to work in the kitchen a lot. I don't remember his name but maybe you will. I know for a fact that he was involved in the rape. They were saying he after everyones was through with you he went down on you. While they were saying this he was standing there licking his lips. The guys that were with him I hadn't seen before. I don't even

Evidence

Ethel C. Richard

Rember what they looked like, or even if they was involved in it.
The next time I saw you, you were sitting on the steps of the church singing. You had just got out of the Hospital, so I went over and asked how you were feeling. You acted like nothing had happened and it really surprised me. I guess sometime its good not to Remember.
Any way thats when we started hanging together. We were together 24 hrs aday untill I was arrested and sent back to Tillamook.
After you came to Tillamook you stayed at the Hotel and worked for a few days at the Fern Cafe. The last time I saw you, you came to my house with a red curly haired guy and told me you were going to a party in Lincoln City. Two days later you called me and said you were going to California to see Bobby.
You wrote me a letter a few weeks later saying you had met someone and was very happy.

Evidence

The Bobby Sherman Miracle

> I'm sorry it took you so long to remember things. I hope this helps put some of your past together. The time we were together was between July & Aug. of 1971. If there's anything else I can do for you please let me know.
>
> Bobby K Sherman
>
> SUBSCRIBED TO AND Sworn before me this 17th day of November, 1995.
>
> Mary R Hansen
> NOTARY PUBLIC FOR Oregon
> My commission expires:
> 5-29-97

Evidence

Ethel C. Richard

Evidence

The Bobby Sherman Miracle

Evidence

Ethel C. Richard

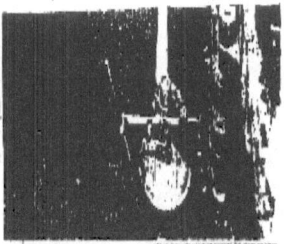

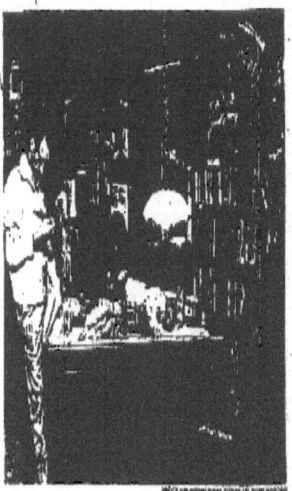

Evidence

The Bobby Sherman Miracle

Hospital / and Bypass
Eye Witness Statement

PSL
Presbyterian/ St. Luke's
Medical Center

1719 East 19th Avenue
Denver, CO 80218
303 869 6000

26 October 1995

To Whom It May Concern:

This is to verify that the records for Ethel C. Richard, d.o.b. 6/19/55 who was a patient at St. Luke's Hospital in either June, July or August of 1971, microfilmed over 20 years ago.

Over the years the microfilm has deteriorated so badly that is is impossible to make any copies. Even trying to read the film on the screen is extremely difficult.

If you have any further questions, please feel free to contact me.

Ken Cort, Supervisor
Health Information Management
Presbyterian/St.Luke's Medical Center
1719 E. 19th Ave.
Denver, Cn 80218

An affiliate of PSL Healthcare System

Evidence

Ethel C. Richard

**SUPERIOR COURT OF CALIFORNIA
COUNTY OF LOS ANGELES
JUVENILE COURT**

PETITION

In the Matter of ETHYL CONSTANCE RICHARDS, a minor

Number 420699-0361434-I DO-NES

New X Active

Petitioner is informed and believes and therefore alleges, that ETHYL CONSTANCE RICHARDS, 250 LAKE AVENUE, MANCHESTER, NEW HAMPSHIRE, hereinafter called minor, resides at 250 LAKE AVENUE, MANCHESTER, NEW HAMPSHIRE, and was born on 6/19/56 and was 14 years of age on 6/19/71, and comes within the provisions of Section 601 of the Welfare and Institutions Code of California, in that:

SAID MINOR IS BEYOND THE CONTROL OF HER PARENTS WITH WHOM SHE RESIDES, IN THAT: ON OR ABOUT JUNE 22, 1971, MINOR WAS FOUND WANDERING WITHOUT A SETTLED PLACE OF ABODE, VISIBLE MEANS OF SUBSISTANCE OR PROPER GUARDIANSHIP WITHIN THIS JURISDICTION. MINOR'S LEGAL RESIDENCE IS WITH HER PARENTS IN MANCHESTER, NEW HAMPSHIRE.

The name and residence address of each parent and guardian of minor, known to me, is as follows:
FATHER: ANDREW A. RICHARDS, 250 LAKE AVENUE, MANCHESTER, NEW HAMPSHIRE
MOTHER: NELLIE J. RICHARDS, SAME

The name and residence address of an adult relative residing within the county, or if there is no such person known, the name and residence address of the adult relative known to me to reside nearest to the court, is:

Minor was taken into custody by BURBANK POLICE DEPARTMENT on 6/22/71 at 5:20 P.M. Minor IS detained. The present whereabouts of minor is JUVENILE HALL.

THEREFORE, petitioner respectfully requests that this minor be adjudged and declared a ward of the Juvenile Court and dealt with as such.

KENNETH E. KIRKPATRICK, PROBATION OFFICER, Petitioner

By A. BUTTS, IDC
Deputy Probation Officer

Evidence

EPILOGUE

This is by no means where the story ends. The real life drama had only begun for Ethel upon being re admitted to NH Hospital in September of 1971 and through the first few years after being discharged from the hospital she would learn more about Ward Sylvester (Bobby's manager) than she realized she should care to learn about. In those years Ward was a man to actually answer his own phones at his office and when Ethel would occasionally get a flicker of memory about being with Bobby (which happened a few times from 1972 to 1979) and would call Ward because she did not have Bobby's number and he would have short talks with Ethel about Bobby and treat Ethel as though she were someone he'd remembered.

Ethel could remember nothing whatsoever about Pecos Jail or her stay at the House of Maranatha, she could not remember Rodney or Denver or Tillamook, Oregon and

Ethel C. Richard

what had happened to her in those places.

The hospital staff had drugged Ethel and she'd been electric shocked and so Ethel could not remember running away…let alone having run away three times and each time making it to California (where her heart was because she really loved Bobby Sherman tremendously and who it turned out after they'd met, had liked Ethel very much as well). However, it was not possible for Ethel to settle and stay in California because Burbank authorities had false information that Ethel was a missing child from NH that needed to be returned to her parents. In reality Ethel had been granted emancipation by a Pecos, Texas juvenile officer who'd investigated her case while he'd had her in custody at Pecos Jail and found the truth that she was not protected by authorities within her home state and that she needed safe haven from authorities there. Having been legally set free by Pecos, Texas authorities, Ethel should never have been taken into custody in Los Angeles.

The only excuse the Los Angeles court had used was her age. She was still fifteen years old when she'd left home the first time. She turned sixteen on June 19, 1971 and was visiting with Bobby the entire day on the set 29 at the Columbia Screen Gems Television Studios Ranch on June 22 (as states the date and time on the Los Angeles Juvenile Court Petition). The television studios ranch is the location where she was taken into custody at 5:20 pm.

That hers was not as crazy a belief that Bobby was her boyfriend (as some had claimed) but that Bobby himself had encouraged her belief because he'd been outwardly

The Bobby Sherman Miracle

affectionate with Ethel in public and had spoken with her on intimate topics and though he'd volunteered (during a personal chat they'd had together) that he could not bring her to his home because it was still not ready, he intimated that he wanted to know her more closely.

Bobby gave to Ethel attention and was obviously flirtatious and openly making remarks and gestures which could be interpreted as an intimate interest (in Ethel's then innocent opinion). Ethel was innocent. Ethel wanted to be Bobby's wife and so why not believe that he was her man? Patty Carnal believed that Bobby was her man and she did marry with Bobby (and Patti was still only seventeen years old when Bobby took her).

Bobby's mom was fifteen when she'd married Bobby's father. Ethel's age would not have come into it (though Bobby was actually twenty eight years old when Ethel was sixteen and they'd been visiting together) however Ethel was from another state and Bobby was a star. Ethel's parents did not like Bobby Sherman or the idea of Ethel living in Los Angeles.

Ethel had never met Patti and had no reason whatsoever to believe that Bobby was seeing anyone.

She'd had good reason to believe that Bobby liked her because Bobby always treated her wonderfully and always gave to her all of his attention while they were together. Even other persons on the grounds of the studios knew that Bobby's eyes were always on Ethel when she was around and he'd been caught eying her and behaving oddly in her presence. None interfered and when Ethel had re appeared again at the studios after having been taken into custody in

Ethel C. Richard

June. Ethel was accepted as a friend and was free to roam the sets as she pleased because she'd been known to be allowed into the sets with Bobby.

Ethel had not been taken into custody at the studios the third time she'd been returned to NH by juvenile authorities in Los Angeles. She'd been taken into custody less than two blocks away from the studios at her girlfriend's home because her girlfriend's mother during a sleepover had wondered about Ethel and at about 8:30 pm called police stating that Ethel appeared to be a minor who had no parents in the area.

Burbank police came to the girlfriend's home and were ready to drop any investigations into Ethel when they saw Ethel had a hospital ID (from St. Luke's Presbyterian Hospital at Denver, Colorado which stated she was eighteen years old). Ethel's friends' mom who was a nurse then told police that anyone could get such an ID and she insisted the police take Ethel into custody.

Ethel was brought to the station and then to juvenile hall. She was returned to NH and the third time not sent directly to her parents' home but kept in custody of juvenile authorities. Bobby married Patti after Ethel had been taken away by authorities however no one had told Ethel about Bob and Patti's marriage.

Ethel was re admitted to the hospital the day after Bobby and Patti's wedding and Bobby and Patti kept their marriage a secret from everyone for a while afterward.

The Discharge Summary from NH Hospital states how little was actually understood about Ethel at that time. She'd not taken drugs but had been poisoned by others

The Bobby Sherman Miracle

with drugs while she'd been in Manhattan, Kansas and Denver, Colorado. The only time she was actually found with drugs in her possession was when she was taken into custody for the second time at the studios ranch and the drugs were a prescription given to her by a physician at Eugene, Oregon (because she had taken seriously ill at Eugene and had collapsed). A resident doctor had taken Ethel into his home and his wife nursed Ethel because the hospital could not admit her, having no beds. Ethel believes that these pills were an antibiotic.

Ethel had done very well in school however she'd not been taken seriously when she'd reported to police and school authorities the behavior of gang elements in her school and in her neighborhood and she'd been falsely accused, misdiagnosed, involuntarily committed to a mental institution, drugged with Mellaril, Thorazine, (and God knows what else) forced into electroshock sessions and then sent back out into the same gang infested neighborhood to fend for herself against those who'd already attacked and terrorized her (and so of course she gave up school and ran away to save her life when no one would help her)!

One more note: The hospital record shows that Ethel had serious memory lapses which were noted within her discharge summary. The memory lapses and episodes of lashing out and flashbacks Ethel experienced while hospitalized were real. They continued for a few years after her discharge. They were caused by factors which could have been entirely avoided because from the very beginning Ethel had refused to take drugs; even the drugs originally prescribed by the

Ethel C. Richard

psychiatrist… she showing anger at his order to take them and telling him that she did not need them.

In a very real and sickening way it was the psychiatrist and the hospital that were directly responsible for any "drug use" by Ethel and what a sham it is that the hospital staff made in any way the inference that Ethel had been guilty of drug abuse!

That Ethel recovered from what had been done to her is a testimony to her strength and resilience and also because she is so strongly against drugs.

Ethel has been totally psychotropic drug free since the early 1970's. She does not ever indulge in alcohol as she does not like it. The last drink she had was two ounces of a Spanish beer in December of 1994 while sitting in a small bar in central Los Angeles.

Before that she'd taken a drink two years prior (a beer) while visiting with a friend (Tom Dae) at his establishment (a popular dance night club) in northern Maine. Ethel's is not the bio of a drug user … it is a bio of one who was poisoned with drugs by others and it is the bio of a survivor who has made it against the odds.

More Evidence

11/2/71

STAFF CONFERENCE

Present: Dr. Kutas, Mrs. Proctor, Mrs. Pemhala, Dr. Bridgette, Mrs. Lucier, Mrs. Smyrl, Mrs. Joan Heath, Mrs. Duffy, Mrs. Mary Sharpe

Ethel, age 16, single, white, Protestant female, was readmitted by order of the Manchester District Court, Juvenile Department, from that Court, residence being Manchester, New Hampshire.

The following observations were noted by Dr. Von Oldenburg: "The patient has run away from home 3 times, has been taking drugs - was unable to keep up with school (8th grade) and finally she was taken to the Juvenile Court who ordered her here. The patient does not agree with the laws of this country. IMP: Personality disorder - antisocial personality."

The parents were interviewed by Mrs. Proctor, Social Worker. Throughout the interview both parents were most cooperative and talked freely about themselves and Ethel.

On September 9th, 1971, Ethel was charged with being a wayward and disobedient child. Ethel was placed at the State Industrial School. She was examined by a psychiatrist and psychologist, both of whom felt that hospitalization was needed.

At the Staff Conference held at the State Industrial School it was felt that Ethel was found to be Schizophrenic, Latent Type. They felt that Ethel was looking for some control and might be motivated to receive psychotherapy. Hospitalization at the New Hampshire Hospital was recommended.

Records reveal that Ethel has a history of being a behavioral problem, and that she has had occasional hallucinatory experiences in childhood which are still present. She has been involved in the use of drugs over the past few years and has also been quite promiscuous.

Parents stated that Ethel has always been a nervous child. As far back as age 8, Ethel talked of becoming an actress. At age 8, Ethel used to dance around the house quite a bit, and it seemed that she lived in her own fantasy world.

Between November 18th and December 18, 1969 Ethel was seen on a private basis by Dr. Koutras who stated that she impressed him as being a schizophrenic adolescent with rather acute onset, a lack of insight and poor motivation for out-patient treatment. On January 6, 1970, Ethel did not show up for her appointment but reported by phone that she was becoming aware of her supernatural capabilities that could prove very important to a university or research center. She was then placed at N. H. Hospital for

PRIVILEGED AND CONFIDENTIAL
DO NOT REDISCLOSE
NEW HAMPSHIRE HOSPITAL

PROGRESS NOTES

PAGE 3
see p. 4

PATIENT IDENTIFICATION

RICHARDS, ETHEL   54322-A
Readm: 9/27/71   Prot.
                     Tobey Building

Ethel C. Richard

DATE	PROGRESS NOTES — All notes to be signed by person making note, and Attending Physician
	STAFF CONFERENCE (Continued)
11/2/71	the first time.

Testing administered March 18, 1970 revealed a Verbal Scale I. Q. of 117, a Performance Scale I. Q. of 93, and a Full Scale I. Q. of 107 on the Wechsler-Bellevue, Form I. She was found to be operating within the average range although she did somewhat better on the verbal scale of the Wechsler, where she shows superiority in abstract thinking and also receives an above average score in practical comprehension. Performance scale scores were average.

On the Behn Rorschach Ethel saw a great many things, was sensitive to human activity, seemed to have a high degree of sensuality and impulsivity. There was some evidence of depressed feelings. In general, the protocol was felt to be overly productive, rather poorly controlled. There seemed to be some denial and hypomanic quality to the test results.

The Mental Status Exam indicated Ethel gave the impression of a mild hypomania. There was almost a press of speech, but she was very spontaneous, quite coherent, and there was no flight of ideas. However, for the most part, what she said remained vaguely outlined. She was well oriented and in good contact.

Interview with Ethel during Staff Conference:

Ethel indicated she felt she had been doing quite well. She stated she had had a couple of flashbacks but is not concerned about them. She would like to get help on the outside and find a job so that she could pay for the bills she has accumulated, i.e. telephone bills, etc. She also has doctor's bills and a plane fare bill.

Ethel has officially quit school. She expressed a great deal of interest in a book she has been reading on cosmology, which she feels is mind expanding. She talked about the "fixed star" and about mirrored images reflected on earth.

Ethel indicates she feels her family is now just starting to communicate, and therefore she is interested in family counseling. She cannot remember any time when her family was not fighting night or day. However, since coming back home, she feels things are better and she is now able to kiss her mother.

Ethel feels she needs therapy to help her with her problem with "dope." "Every time she thinks about grass, she would like to have some." She feels she should be allowed to go home even though she still has flashbacks because they are not bad, only once or twice a month. "I am naturally tripping all the time, but I can do about anything as I can handle it." When she is

Continued

PAGE 6 — see p. 5

PRIVILEGED AND CONFIDENTIAL
DO NOT REDISCLOSE
NEW HAMPSHIRE HOSPITAL
PROGRESS NOTES

PATIENT IDENTIFICATION
RICHARD, Ethel
Readm: 9/27/71
54322-A
Prot.
Tobey Building

FORM NO. MED-REC. 32 REV 9/88 (2/69)

Evidence

The Bobby Sherman Miracle

DATE	PROGRESS NOTES
	All notes to be signed by person making note, and Attending Physician
11/2/71	STAFF CONFERENCE (Continued) tripping, she gets "a tipsie feeling, distorted senses, and all of a sudden I feel really good." Ethel would like to be discharged, find herself a job, save some money so that when she is eighteen she will return to California to look up her friends, and particularly her boyfriend. She talked about her friend Bobby Sherman and about how people do not believe her about him. She claims she called him a couple weeks ago, and asked him why he was not writing her, and said he does not have time. He has not visited her because of the tight schedule he has. **Discussion:** Dr. Kuten was impressed with the fact that there were no signs of schizophrenia in the testing. Although there was a great deal of verbalization, the content was not bizarre. The staff wondered about the stories Ethel tells with regard to having a boyfriend, Bobby Sherman, about visiting him, etc. whether or not these are false. Dr. Kuten indicated there was no evidence of thought disorganization except for manic responses at times, and he felt that she had improved and essentially was not psychotic. Dr. Kuten did not feel we would be able to rehabilitate her. The teacher indicated that in class Ethel is many times in a world of her own. The staff did not know what they could do for Ethel. They did feel that there is more communication between Ethel and her parents than there was before. Mrs. Smyrl did not feel Ethel was capable of holding down a job. **Recommendations:** The staff agreed that we could go along with Ethel's desires, that is, discharge her, arranging for family counselling, and find employment. A report to the court. **Diagnosis:** Adjustment Reaction of Adolescence. **Prognosis:** Guarded. Jay Kuten, M.D. Consultant Psychiatrist

PAGE 5
SEE PG. 6

NEW HAMPSHIRE HOSPITAL
PROGRESS NOTES
PRIVILEGED CONFIDENTIAL
DO NOT REDISCLOSE

PATIENT IDENTIFICATION
RICHARD, Ethel   54322-A
Readm: 9/27/71   Prot.
                   Tobey Building

Evidence

Ethel C. Richard

DATE	PROGRESS NOTES — All notes to be signed by person making note, and Attending Physician
2/10/71 as of visit of 12/3/71	**DISCHARGE SUMMARY** Readmission of a 16-year-old white, single, Protestant female on a Juvenile District Court Order from the Manchester District Court. She was readmitted to N.H. Hospital because of taking drugs, unable to keep up with school and running away from home 3 times. Ethel comes from an intact family, being the oldest of 3 children. Both Mr. & Mrs. Richards have been married before. They both state they are happy with each other and are both in agreement about Ethel's behavior and emotional problems. Mrs. Richard is a housewife and Mr. Richards works at the Modern Appliance Furniture Store which is operated by his brother. Parents reported that Ethel has no particular health problem at the present time. She has always had difficulty in school, was a behavior problem in school and has not yet finished the 8th grade. In Junior High School she was disruptive because she was constantly making up stories. In the 8th grade she told school authorities that she was pregnant. On September 9, 1971, Ethel was charged with being a wayward and disobedient child. She was placed at the State Industrial School and was examined by a psychiatrist and psychologist. Both felt that hospitalization was needed. Records reveal that Ethel has a history of being a behavioral problem, and that she has had occasional hallucinatory experiences in childhood which are yet present. She has been involved in the use of drugs over the past few years and has also been quite promiscuous. Mental Status Examination revealed Ethel to be very spontaneous, quite coherent and in no sense is there any flight of ideas, although what she says remains vaguely outlined. There is almost a press of speech. She gives the impression of a mild hyopmania. She is well oriented and in good contact. There are mild cognitive deficiencies, but these are not severe. Psychological testing included the Binet Vocabulary, Wechsler Bellevue, Form I: Verbal Scale I.Q. 117, Performance Scale I.Q. 93 and full scale I.Q. 107, Behn Rorschach and the T.A.T. These tests reveal Ethel to show superiority in abstract thinking in which she gave clear and capable answers. Ethel exhibited an average capability, but more than the usual amount of verbalization. There seemed to be some denial and hypomanic quality to the test results. On admission Ethel was quiet and cooperative—showing bizarre behavior—sitting in a corner singing for long intervals, extremely loud—writing letters to singing stars in Hollywood. She had numerous physical complaints which, when checked, were negative. She did not get along well with the other girls, was very critical and making threats. She started in school—acted quite oddly at times—incoherent conversations—has had a couple of episodes of screaming and memory lapse which she claims are "flashbacks". No noticeable change in condition. Day visits with parents were started and she handled these very well, and eventually these were extended into weekend visits which went good. She had very poor personal hygiene, dressed badly and didn't particulary care how she smelled or looked. Did fairly well in school, but still didn't get along very well with the other girls or with the staff.

PAGE 6
SEE PAGE 7

PATIENT IDENTIFICATION
RICHARDS, Ethel   54322-A
Readm: 9/27/71   Prot.

Tobey 1

FORM NO. MED. REC. 32 REV 9/68 (2/69)

Evidence

The Bobby Sherman Miracle

DATE	PROGRESS NOTES
12/10/71	Discharge Summary cont.
	Psychiatric Diagnosis: ADJUSTMENT REACTION OF ADOLESCENCE.
	Physical Diagnosis: NONE.
	Manifestations: Runaway, drug use, problems in school.
	Condition: Improved.
	Prognosis: Guarded.
	Psychiatric Incapacity: Moderate.
	Recommendations: To be discharged to the home of her parents, get a job, be kept on probation and if any problems should arise, they should seek help from the Manchester Guidance Clinic.
	Medication: None.
	Destination: To the home of her parents:
	Mr. & Mrs. Andrew Richards
	250 Lake Avenue
	Manchester, New Hampshire

[signature]
Pierre O. Durand, M.D.
Director of Children's Services

POD:st

NEW HAMPSHIRE HOSPITAL
PROGRESS NOTES

PAGE 7

PATIENT IDENTIFICATION

RICHARDS, Ethel   54322-A
Readm: 9/27/71   Prot.

Tobey 1

FORM NO. MED. REC. 32 REV 9/RR (2/69)

Evidence

Ethel C. Richard

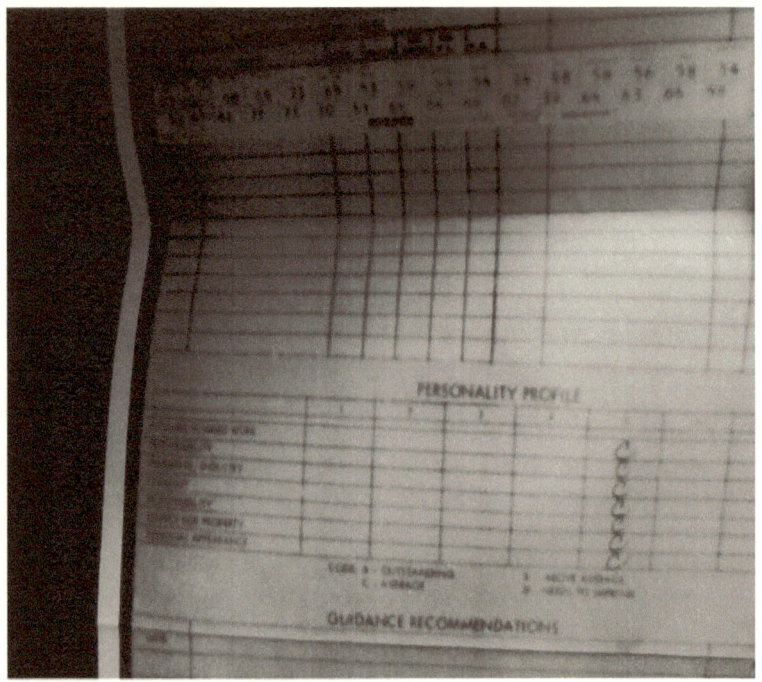

What part of "Ethel had average to good behavior and an above average intelligence as a child" did the psychiatrist Cristos Koutras not understand? It may have helped him to get accurate information about Ethel from Ethel's school records!

Evidence

The Bobby Sherman Miracle

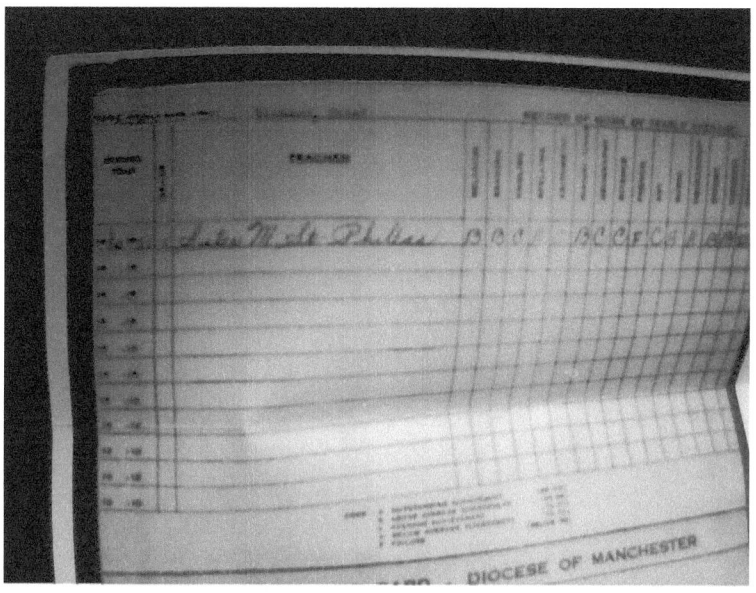

Notice Ethel's grades in fifth grade. Not too shabby except for the F in french. Ethel hated french. The dean of the school did not mind that Ethel failed french and he commended her for her other grades in front of the class because she'd studied hard and been the winner of the fifth grade parochial school spelling bees for NH and was given the honor of representing all fifth grade parochial school students within the state at the national spelling bees in Washington that year. Ethel was eleven years old. (1966)

Evidence

Ethel C. Richard

Evidence

www.ingramcontent.com/pod-product-compliance
Lightning Source LLC
Chambersburg PA
CBHW020108020526
44112CB00033B/1095